Berlitz®

Ireland

Front cover: Ballydonegan Bay,
County Cork
Above: The *Hands Across the Divide*
monument in Derry

TOP 10 ATTRACTIONS

Glendalough An ancient monastery in a spectacular setting *(page 44)*

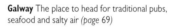

Galway The place to head for traditional pubs, seafood and salty air *(page 69)*

Book of Kells Trinity College, Dublin, houses wonderfully ornate pro of Ireland's monastic he *(page 28)*

Dingle Peninsula This finger of land lives up to visitors' romantic notio Ireland *(page 63)*

range These burial chambers represent a major feat of historic engineering (page 40)

Cork City The Republic's second city has an old-fashioned charm (page 54)

n Liquor Saloon t's foremost pub has a ficent tiled interior and fully carved private (page 83)

Donegal The county's countryside and coastline have a wild beauty that hasn't been spoiled by tourism (page 78)

n Street Dublin's ing artery has a ental air (page 28)

Temple Bar The lively hub of Dublin's nightlife (page 34)

A PERFECT TOUR

Day 1   Dublin

Walk the streets of Georgian Dublin, from Trinity College's cobbled quadrangle to the wide expanse of Merrion Square, then enjoy a light lunch at the National Gallery. Cross the Ha'penny Bridge and follow O'Connell Street to Parnell Square and the Dublin Writers Museum.

Day 3   Cork City

Explore Cork's city centre on foot, lunching in the vast covered food market. Then take a 20-minute train ride to the port of Cobh, the last sight of home for generations of emigrants, whose tale is told at The Queenstown Story visitor centre.

Day 4   Killarney

The west Cork coastal road (N71) meanders through tiny villages whe the pubs showcase local artisan foods, to the treasure-packed Bantry House and sub-tropical Glengarriff. Drive throug Kenmare to Moll's Gap f a jaw-droppingly scenic approach to Killarney.

Day 2   Kilkenny and Tipperary

Leave Dublin by car for Kilkenny, founded by St Canice in the 6th century, and Kilkenny Castle, a magnificent edifice in rich parkland beside the River Nore. Have lunch at the Kilkenny Design Centre, an emporium of Irish crafts. Drive on to Tipperary and climb the Rock of Cashel, to savour its magnificent ruins.

Day 5 & 6   Kerry

Explore the deep blue lakes and heather-clad mountains of Killarney o foot, by bicycle, or pony and trap. The Gap of Dunloe excursion includ a lake cruise, which can joined at Ross Castle.

OF IRELAND

Day 8 **The wild west**

...rive west from Galway to Connemara, a sparsely ...pulated wilderness of bog, scattered blue lakes and ...stant purple mountains. Enjoy the seafood in Clifden, ...en head for the Connemara National Park, and walk up ...amond Hill for a panoramic view.

Day 10 **Belfast**

An impressive Victorian city with chic bars and restaurants, and quirky museums and libraries, Belfast is a popular weekend break destination, with friendly locals, known for their down-to-earth sense of humour. Take a boat tour around its docks to explore the history of the Titanic, and understand the local pride in the city's industrial past.

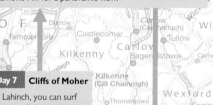

Day 7 **Cliffs of Moher**

... Lahinch, you can surf ...e same Atlantic breakers ...at pound the nearby ...ffs of Moher. Warm ...with Irish stew in ...oolin while foot-tapping ...live Irish music, and ...nsider a day trip to the ...an Islands, or a visit to ...e Burren's numerous ...egalithic remains.

Day 9 **The Antrim Coast**

Wonder at the Giant's Causeway's bizarre basalt columns, as have generations of visitors. Enjoy the cosy inn at Bushmills, next door to Ireland's oldest distillery *(see page 106)*. Nearby are the romantic ruins of Dunluce Castle, perched on a clifftop.

CONTENTS

24

61

95

92

52

81

INTRODUCTION

The grass really does grow greener in Ireland – it's not called the 'Emerald Isle' for nothing, although the rain-drenched verdant pastures alternate with plains of grain, bleak and rugged hills, mountains and soggy bogs. The quick-changing sky adds to the drama of the encounter between land and sea. You will never be further than 115km (70 miles) from Ireland's dramatic 4,800-km (3,000-mile) coastline. Far to the west lies America, a beacon for countless emigrants during the 19th century. To the east lies Britain, whose relationship with its next-door neighbour has for 800 years been one of the most infuriatingly complex in European geopolitics.

The proximity of the Gulf Stream keeps winters mild. Snow is rare, rain is not. Significant rainfall is recorded on three out of every four days near the west coast, and on every second day in the east, and ranges from stormy torrents to refreshing mist so nebulous that it leaves the pavement unmarked. The sun is never far behind the rain, however, and the slightest shower has always been a fine excuse for an Irish rainbow.

Emigration

Around 6 million people live on the island – fewer than before the great potato famine of the 1840s. Emigration was high until the 'Celtic Tiger' boom, when jobs in new industries kept locals at home. With the bleaker economic outlook people are leaving again.

There are, of course, two Irelands: the 26 counties of the Republic of Ireland (Éire) and the six counties of Northern Ireland. This gives the island two capitals: Dublin and Belfast. In Dublin, a lively city of broad avenues, green parks and harmonious, ordered terraces,

Wild horses in Connemara, Co Galway

there is more in the way of museums, galleries and other cultural attractions than in many cities of comparable size, plus a delightfully subversive sense of humour that some would say conceals a deep sense of fatalism. In contrast, Belfast is Ireland's only industrial centre and its energy is more grounded and less subtle than Dublin's.

By and large, though, the truly inspiring sights of Ireland are found outside the big towns. Ireland is still rooted in agriculture and, as you travel by car or bus from one town to the next, you will pass through miles of farmland generously populated with sheep and cattle. Natural wonders in Ireland can be as awesome as the Cliffs of Moher, or as tranquil as the Lakes of Killarney; as mystical as the holy mountain of Croagh Patrick, or as delightful as the horse-breeding pastures of the Curragh. Scattered amidst these natural beauties stand impressive stone relics which date back thousands of years. In Ireland, the concept of a town is not much more than a thousand years old. Before then, the island was almost entirely rural, and its now ancient buildings often began as monastic settlements that kept learning alive in Europe during the Dark Ages.

This is a small country but, like vintage wine, it should be savoured slowly. A signpost may present you with three ways

Where There's Smoke

The characteristic smell of peat fires pervades much of Ireland's countryside. Since the 17th century the bogs have been exploited as an inexpensive source of fuel. During the great potato famine (1845–51) dried peat was often the only fuel available. In recent times, more efficient methods of cutting the peat have put an extra strain on Irish bogs and, although peat fires smell lovely in winter, the remaining bogs are to be protected from further digging.

of getting to a destination, or it may show none. Ask a passer-by, and, if they decide you look a bit weary after a hard day's sightseeing and comparing pints of Guinness, they'll probably reassure you that it's 'just a wee way ahead' because they won't wish to distress you by telling you it's really 32km (20 miles) by a narrow, twisting road.

The Irish

There is no single 'Irish' character. The Northern Protestant is generally regarded as being more earnest and less imaginative than the Northern Catholic,

The Cliffs of Moher in Co Clare

who in turn is seen as more introverted and less impulsive than the Southern Catholic. The Irish refine these distinctions even further, giving the sense of place an importance seldom found elsewhere in the world.

More than 1.8 million people live in Dublin, the largest city in the Republic of Ireland and home to almost a third of its population. Belfast, with a population of around 650,000, is the hub of Northern Ireland, which remained a part of the United Kingdom when the island was partitioned after World War I. The new republic, whose birth pangs in 1922 included a civil war, settled down to being a predominantly rural economy, with social affairs and its education system strongly influenced by the Roman Catholic church.

In the final quarter of the 20th century, as Northern Ireland was suffering political turmoil, the South set about transforming itself into a modern European state. Membership of the European Union provided great economic benefits, and tax incentives were strategically used to attract European and American industries, primarily in the high-tech and pharmaceutical sectors. The old taboos on divorce and sex outside marriage began to fade away as the influence of the church declined. A strong youth culture turned Dublin into a party town targeted for weekend breaks by Europe's budget airlines.

A Native Tongue

The historic Anglo-Norman conquest of Ireland in 1169 paved the way for the supremacy of the English language over Gaelic. Nowadays, scarcely one in a hundred people in Ireland speaks

Enjoying the Guinness Storehouse

Irish with some degree of fluency. However, reviving Gaelic – or Irish, as it is usually called, has become state policy; it is taught in schools and printed (along with English) on all official signs and documents. Indeed, in some Gaelic-speaking (Gaeltacht) areas now, road signs are in Gaelic only, which can make life difficult for tourists. Everyday

Gaelic pub sign

use of Gaelic is limited to these areas. Its vocabulary, intonation and sentence structures have infiltrated English, creating great literature and lending everyday speech patterns a touch of poetry.

The Northern Counties

For the last three decades of the 20th century, the image of Northern Ireland was blighted by terrorists, who aspired to unite its six counties with the Republic's 26. Today, although tribal animosities can still be ignited, a somewhat tetchy harmony prevails much of the time and the substantial subsidies poured into the region from Britain, the European Union and the United States have created a relative prosperity.

Two things have been insufficiently appreciated: the down-to-earth friendliness of the people (towards outsiders, anyway) and the spectacular scenery – any other country combining the allure of the Antrim Coast Road, the Giant's Causeway, the lakes of Fermanagh, the Mountains of Mourne and a wealth of golf courses would sink under the weight of tourists. But, in the end, confounding expectations is something at which both parts of the island effortlessly excel.

A BRIEF HISTORY

Stone-Age relics reveal that Ireland has been inhabited for at least 8,000 years. The first settlers probably travelled on foot from Scandinavia to Scotland – England was linked at that time to northern Europe by land – then across what was a narrow sea gap to Ireland.

During the late Stone Age, inhabitants began to settle down and farm. Tombs and temples from this period can be found across the country. These monuments may be simple stone tripods in the middle of a farmer's field, or they can be sophisticated passage-graves built on astronomical principles and decorated with mysterious spiral and zigzag engravings.

Portrait of Christ from the 9th-century Book of Kells

New settlers introduced Bronze-Age skills from Europe, but by the time of the Iron Age Ireland was lagging behind the Continent. This technology did not reach the island until the last years of the pre-Christian era, thanks to Celtic tribes from central Europe.

The Roman legions that rolled across Western Europe into Britain stopped short at the Irish Sea. The island was left free to develop its own way of life during the centuries of the great Roman Empire. Though Irish society was decentralised into scores of bickering mini-kingdoms, a single culture did develop. Druids and poets told legends in a common language that is clearly recognisable as the Irish version of Gaelic.

St Patrick's Day

The Celts frequently staged raids on Roman Britain for booty and slaves. During one 5th-century raid, they rounded up a large number of captives to ease the manpower shortage. One of these 'immigrants', a 16-year-old boy named Patrick, later became Ireland's national saint. After spending a few years as a humble shepherd, he escaped to Gaul, became a monk, and finally returned to convert 'the heathens' to Christianity.

St Patrick and his successors developed a system of monasteries to serve as the centre for all church activities. This suited life in Ireland – a rural and scantly populated island. While the rest of Europe crawled through the Dark Ages, the Irish monasteries kept the flame of Western culture alight. Scholarly minds from different regions of Europe converged on the island to participate in its religious and intellectual life. The monks from the 'island of saints and scholars' created beautiful illuminated manuscripts while others travelled to Britain and mainland Europe, founding monasteries abroad.

The Vikings

At the turn of the 9th century, well-armed warriors sailed in from Scandinavia aboard sleek boats. The undefended Irish monasteries, full of relics and treasures, were easy targets. The shallow-draught ships moved in and attacked virtually at will, making their way around the Irish coast and up its rivers as well. This danger inspired multi-storey 'round towers', which variously served as watchtowers, belfries, storehouses, and escape hatches. The remains of over 70 still stand. But plunder wasn't the only thing on the Viking agenda: they soon added trading colonies around the coast and founded the first towns on the rural island – Dublin, Waterford and Limerick.

The Irish learned sailing, weaponry and metalworking from the Norse, but resented their presence. In the end, the natives ousted the Vikings, with the last struggle taking place in 1014 at the Battle of Clontarf, when the High King of Ireland, Brian Ború, defeated the tough Norse and their Irish allies, although he himself was killed in the battle.

Ireland's Viking heritage is remembered in Dublin

Rivalry and Revenge

Ireland's next invasion was motivated by jealousy. In 1152, the wife of Tiernan O'Rourke, an Irish warrior king, was carried off by rival Dermot MacMurrough of Leinster. Allegedly the lady was a willing victim, possibly even the instigator. Regardless, O'Rourke got his queen back a few months later, but wasn't about to forgive and forget. He forced Dermot to flee, in 1166, first to England and then France. But from there, Dermot was able to shape an alliance with a powerful Norman nobleman, the Earl of Pembroke. The Earl, known as Strongbow, agreed to lead an army to sweep Dermot back to power. In exchange, the Earl was to be given the hand of Dermot's daughter and the right to succeed him to the Leinster throne. The hardy Normans – the elite of Europe's warriors – won the Battle of Waterford in 1169, and Strongbow married his princess in Waterford's grand cathedral.

In further engagements, the Norman war machine stunned and swiftly defeated Norse and Irish forces. Things were going so well for Strongbow that his overlord, King Henry II of England, arrived in 1171 to assert his sovereignty.

The English Ascendancy

The Anglo-Norman occupation brought profound and long-lasting changes. Towns, churches and castles were built alongside institutions for feudal government. There was much resentment among the Irish, but for the colonial rulers the challenge of revolt was less serious than the danger of total cultural assimilation. With settlers adopting the ways of the natives, rather than the other way round, the Statutes of Kilkenny were introduced in 1366, banning intermarriage and forbidding the English from speaking Gaelic.

English control was consolidated when the House of Tudor turned its attention to Ireland. Henry VIII, the first English monarch to be titled 'King of Ireland', introduced the Reformation to Ireland as well as England, but the new religion of Protestantism took root only in the Pale (the area around Dublin) and in the large provincial towns under English control. In the rest of Ireland, Catholic monasteries carried on as before, as did the Irish language.

From the mid-16th century, the implementation of the so-called plantation policy heralded the large-scale redistribution of wealth. Desirable farmland was confiscated from Catholics and given to Protestant settlers. During the Reign of Elizabeth I revolts were widespread, but the most unyielding resistance was in the northeastern province of Ulster, where chiefs

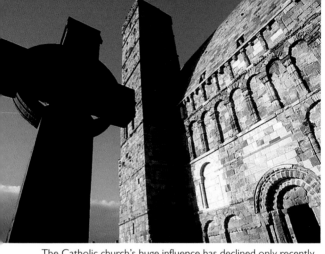

The Catholic church's huge influence has declined only recently

formed an alliance with Spain – the Queen's bitterest enemy. In 1601, a Spanish mini-armada sailed into the southern port of Kinsale. The English defeated the invaders and the Ulstermen who attempted to join them. Leading Ulster aristocrats, now defeated, abandoned their land for European exile. The 'plantation' programme continued fitfully. During the reign of James I, most of the northern land was confiscated and 'planted' with thousands of Scots and English, who changed the face of the province. After the English Civil War, Oliver Cromwell, England's ruler, ruthlessly massacred the garrisons at Drogheda and Wexford as the price for their support of Charles I, and pursued his own colonisation of Ireland. From 1654, Catholics were only allowed to hold land west of the River Shannon, much of it scarcely habitable. 'To Hell or Connaught' was the slogan used to sum up the alternatives for the dispossessed.

After the religious war that culminated in the Battle of the Boyne *(see box)*, the Irish Catholic majority was subjected to further persecution in the form of the Penal Laws, introduced by the all-Protestant Irish parliament and designed to keep Catholics away from positions of power and influence.

Revolutionary Ideas

It took the American Revolution to provoke daring new thinking in Ireland. Henry Grattan led agitation for greater freedom and tolerance. A Protestant of aristocratic heritage, he staunchly defended in the House of Commons in London the rights of all Irishmen. Further pressure came from an Irish Protestant, Theobald Wolfe Tone, a young lawyer campaigning for parliamentary reform and the abolition of anti-Catholic laws. In 1793 Catholic landholders won the vote and other concessions thanks to Tone. In 1798 a French squadron came to the aid of Tone's United Irishmen off the coast of Cork. It was swiftly intercepted by British naval forces and Wolfe Tone was captured. Convicted of treason, he cut his own throat before his sentence of death by hanging could be carried out.

In 1801 the Irish Parliament voted itself out of business by approving the Act of Union which established the United Kingdom of Great Britain and Ireland. All Irish MPs would now

Battle of the Boyne

Ireland became the battleground for an English power struggle when William of Orange, a Dutchman and a Protestant, challenged his father-in-law, the Catholic James II, for the British throne. From exile in France, James sailed to Ireland to mobilise allies and met William's army in July 1690 at the River Boyne. The Orangemen, aided by troops from several Protestant countries, vastly outnumbered the Irish and French forces. As battles go, it set no records for scope or tactical innovation. But the anniversary of William's victory is still celebrated with fervour by Protestants in Northern Ireland.

The Liberator

Daniel O'Connell was one of the first Irish Catholics to qualify as a barrister, and went on to secure the repeal of anti-Catholic legislation in 1829, giving him the name 'the Liberator'.

sit at Westminster. In 1823 Daniel O'Connell founded the Catholic Association to work for emancipation. Five years later, he won a seat in the House of Commons, but as a Catholic was legally forbidden to take it. To prevent conflict, Parliament passed the Emancipation Act (1829), removing the most discriminatory laws.

Starvation and Emigration

One of the worst disasters of 19th-century Europe was the Great Famine. The problem emerged in September 1845, when potato blight was found on farms in southeast Ireland. The British government set up an investigation, but the outbreak was misdiagnosed. The next crop failed nationwide, wiping out the staple food of the Irish peasant. Cruel winter weather and the outbreak of disease added to the horror of starvation. Believing that they should not interfere with free market forces, the British government did not provide relief.

Survivors fled the stricken land aboard creaking 'coffin ships'. Irish refugees swamped towns such as Liverpool, Halifax, Boston and New York. The famine reduced the population of Ireland by two million – half dying, the rest emigrating. It took another century for the decline in population figures to be reversed and the flow of emigrants stemmed.

Frustration and Revolt

At the end of the 19th century Nationalist sentiment grew and in 1905 a number of nationalist groups were consolidated in a movement called Sinn Féin ('We Ourselves').

The Easter Rising of 1916 rebels seized the General Post Office in Dublin and declared Ireland's independence from

Britain. The authorities crushed the rising, which had lacked support, but their pitiless execution of the ringleaders reversed public opinion. The fight for independence had begun.

At the next general election the nationalist Sinn Féin, led by Eamon de Valera, won by a landslide. The newly elected Sinn Féin parliamentarians refused to take their seats in the Commons in London, but set themselves up in Dublin as Dáil Éireann, the new parliament of Ireland.

More than two years of guerrilla warfare followed until the partition of Ireland was agreed in December 1921. Under it, six counties of the north, where the Protestant majority rejected rule from Dublin, were allowed to remain part of the United Kingdom. The other 26 counties had a Catholic majority and became the Irish Free State (Éire), a dominion within the British Empire. The British hoped that the two sides would soon patch up their differences, but few republicans accepted the settlement and a bitter civil war broke out in the South, lasting until 1923. Nine years later Eamon de Valera came to power, vowing to reinstate the ancient Gaelic language and culture. The 26 counties remained neutral in World War II and formally became an independent republic in 1949.

Emigration statue, County Cork

Britain left Northern Ireland to its own devices and its own government. Many Catholics did not recognise the province's legitimacy, and many Protestants responded by ensuring that jobs and public housing went mainly to Protestants. In 1969 civil rights marches against these injustices were repressed, unleashing old hatreds in waves of terrorism that lasted for three decades. The Good Friday Agreement, signed in 1998, established the framework for a self-governing Northern Ireland. In 2005, the IRA declared a permanent ceasefire and decommissioned its weapons preparing the way for the formation of a new government in May 2007.

In 2002, Ireland was one of the first twelve countries to adopt the euro. With the creation of new industries and huge investment in infrastructure, the 'Celtic Tiger' roared. Then, in the wake of the global financial crisis, Ireland entered a severe recession. Unregulated deals between bankers and property developers created a multi-billion euro banking debt. The centre-right Fianna Fail party under Taoiseach Brian Cowen decided that the State would take on the bankers' debts, and imposed a series of swingeing pay cuts and tax hikes all round. The party lost the 2011 election resoundingly, and a coalition government under Enda Kenny assumed power. The historic visit of Her Majesty Queen Elizabeth II in May 2011, in which she laid a wreath in the Garden of Remembrance alongside President Mary McAleese in a widely appreciated gesture of reconciliation, was a beacon of hope in a bleak economic landscape. But Irish spirits remain high, in spite of economic doom, spurred on by the popular mantra, 'Keep going, sure it's grand.'

Taoiseach Enda Kenny

Historical Landmarks

c.7000BC Date of earliest archaeological evidence along the coast.

c.500BC Celts migrate to Britain. Ireland's Iron Age begins.

c.432 St Patrick converts Ireland to Christianity.

1014 Brian Ború, High King of Ireland, defeats Vikings near Clontarf.

1366 Statutes of Kilkenny forbid English to intermarry or speak Gaelic.

1541 Henry VIII declares himself King of Ireland.

1608 James I moves Protestant Scots and English to Ulster Plantation.

1649 Oliver Cromwell conquers Ireland in a merciless campaign.

1690 William of Orange defeats England's Catholic King James II at the Battle of the Boyne.

1800 Act of Union makes Ireland part of the United Kingdom.

1845–51 The Great Potato Famine; over 1 million people die.

1905 Sinn Féin ('We Ourselves') is formed.

1916 James Connolly and Pádraig Pearse lead 1,800 volunteers who occupy public buildings in the 'Easter Rising'.

1918–23 Sinn Féin wins a landslide of seats in parliament and forms Irish parliament in Dublin. After the 1919–21 Anglo-Irish War, the treaty creates the Irish Free State, excluding the six counties of Northern Ireland.

1937 The Free State, Éire, adopts its own constitution.

1949 Having remained neutral in World War II, Éire leaves the British Commonwealth and becomes the Republic of Ireland.

1972 British soldiers shoot dead 13 demonstrators on 'Bloody Sunday'. Belfast's parliament is dissolved. Northern Ireland is ruled from London.

1973 The Republic of Ireland joins the EEC (now the European Union).

1998 The Good Friday Agreement is signed in Northern Ireland.

2002 The Republic of Ireland adopts the euro.

2007 A united government is formed in Northern Ireland.

2010 Having gone into recession in the global financial crisis, the collapse of two Irish banks creates a national debt of over 24 billion euros.

2011 After the collapse of the Fianna Fail government, a coalition government is formed by Fine Gael and Labour. Queen Elizabeth II pays her first visit to Ireland. Michael D. Higgins is elected as Ireland's President.

WHERE TO GO

The best way to see Ireland is by car, though various package deals or bus tours exist as an alternative. You can see a good deal of the country using public transport, although apart from the main routes, the bus schedules are designed more for country folk than tourists.

This book covers the highlights of the Republic and Northern Ireland, starting in Dublin and proceeding clockwise. We cannot describe all the sights – or all the counties – but wherever you go, you'll enjoy Ireland best at an unhurried Irish pace.

DUBLIN

The Republic of Ireland's capital (pop. over 1.8 million) is the birthplace and inspiration of many great authors, and an elegant European city with many outstanding examples of 18th-century architecture. **Dublin ❶** is pervaded by contrasting moods; from its noble avenues and intimate side streets to chic shopping and traditional pubs, there are also museums, colleges and plenty of sports. In this melting pot of old and new, traditional lace still masks modern windows.

> **What's in a name?**
>
> The city's name comes from the Irish 'Dubh Linn', meaning 'a dark pool'. The much older Gaelic name, 'Baile Atha Cliath', means 'the town of the hurdle ford'.

O'Connell Street to St Stephen's Green

The main avenue in Dublin is **O'Connell Street**. Measuring 46m (150ft) across, it has five monuments to Irish history

The statue of James Joyce off O'Connell Street

lined along the middle. The Millennium Spire, a 395-foot high stainless steel monument, replaced the 19th-century Nelson's Pillar blown up by anti-British rebels in 1966.

O'Connell Street's most famous landmark is the **General Post Office**. The GPO was the command post of the 1916 Easter Rising and was badly damaged in the fighting. A plaque on the front of the building and paintings inside mark the event.

Just opposite O'Connell Bridge is the imposing monument honouring 'The Liberator', Daniel O'Connell (1775–1847, *see page 20*), after whom both the street and bridge are named.

From the bridge, wider than it is long, you can look up and down the **River Liffey** and along the embankments. To the east, rises the copper dome of the 18th-century **Custom House**. Like many buildings along the Liffey, it was badly

Dublin's Ha'penny Bridge at night

damaged in the civil war of 1921. Further east lies the shiny new IFSC (Irish Financial Services Centre), gateway to the high-rise Docklands area, with modern apartments and the 2,000-seater Grand Canal Theatre. To the west is the **Ha'penny Bridge**, so called because that's what it originally cost to cross it.

Fellows Square and the Old Library at Trinity College

The imposing white building facing College Green on the south side of the River Liffey is a branch of the **Bank of Ireland**, originally home of the Irish parliament in the 18th century. The bank moved in when parliament was abolished by the Act of Union in 1801 *(see page 19)*.

Behind the railings at the entrance to **Trinity College** are the statues of two famous alumni – philosopher Edmund Burke and playwright Oliver Goldsmith. Founded by Queen Elizabeth I in 1592, Trinity is a timeless enclave of calm and scholarship in the middle of this bustling city. For centuries it was an exclusively Protestant institution, and as recently as 1956 the Catholic church forbade its students to attend Trinity 'under pain of mortal sin'. Today, TCD, as it is called, is integrated. Students lead informative college tours from a desk at the front porch (mid-May–Sept Mon–Sat, every 40 minutes from 10.15am).

The campus forms a monument to the good taste of the 18th century, and visitors enjoy cobbled walks among trimmed lawns, fine old trees, statues and stone buildings. You can also enjoy art exhibitions at the Douglas Hyde Gallery, and the child-friendly Science Gallery.

The greatest treasures are in the vaulted Long Room in the **Old Library** (May–Sept Mon–Sat 9.30am–5pm, Sun 9.30–4.30pm, Oct–Apr Mon–Sat 9.30am–5pm, Sun noon–4.30pm; charge; www.tcd.ie), where double-decker shelving holds thousands of books published prior to 1800, and priceless early manuscripts are displayed in glass cases. In the adjacent Colonnades Gallery, queues of tourists reverently wait for a look at the **Book of Kells**. This 340-page parchment wonder, handwritten and illustrated by monks during the 9th century, contains a Latin version of the New Testament. The beauty of the script – the illumination (the decoration of initial letters and words) – and the bright abstract designs make this the most wonderful treasure to survive from Ireland's Golden Age. The vellum leaves are turned every day to protect them from light and to give visitors a chance to come back for more.

A left turn on leaving Trinity by the main gate brings you to the entrance of **Grafton Street Ⓑ**, the main shopping and social artery of the city's southside. More than anywhere else, Grafton Street demonstrates Dublin's knack for seeming to bustle and dawdle at the same time. Buskers entertain passers-by on their way to the famous Brown Thomas department store and other shopping emporiums, such as the stunning Powerscourt Townhouse Centre or the massive Stephen's Green Shopping Centre at the south end.

Examples of Europe's finest Georgian houses can be seen facing **Merrion Square**. The discreet, smart brick houses have Georgian doorways flanked by tall columns and topped by fanlights. No two are alike. In a complex of formal buildings on the west side of the square stands the city's largest 18th-century mansion, home of the Duke of Leinster. Today **Leinster House** is the seat of the Irish parliament, which consists of the Senate (*Seanad Éireann*) and the Chamber of Deputies (the *Dáil*, pronounced 'doyle'); and just north of here on Merrion Square West is the National Gallery.

At the entrance to the **National Gallery**  (Mon–Sat 9.30am–5.30pm, Thur until 8.30pm, Sun noon–5.30pm; free; www.nationalgallery.ie) you will see a statue of George Bernard Shaw, famous and respected Dubliner known locally as a benefactor of the institution. In the gallery, some 2,000 works of art are displayed. Irish artists receive priority, but other nationalities are well represented, such as Dutch, English, Flemish, French, Italian and Spanish masters, including Fra' Angelico, Rubens, Rembrandt, Canaletto, Gainsborough and Goya.

Buskers on Grafton Street

Recent additions include a work by Van Gogh and the gallery's first Renoir.

The main entrance to the **National Museum of Archaeology and History** (Tue–Sat 10am–5pm, Sun 2–5pm; free; www.museum.ie), a Dublin institution, is reached from Kildare Street. Its collection of Irish antiquities holds several surprises, from old skeletons and tools to exquisite gold ornaments of the Bronze Age. Famous items include the 8th-century Ardagh Chalice, the delicate Tara Brooch from the same era and the 12th-century Shrine of St Patrick's Bell. You can also see ancient Ogham stones and replicas of the greatest carved stone crosses from the early centuries of Christian Ireland.

Dublin is well-endowed with squares and parks. The biggest of these – and possibly the biggest city square in Europe – is the famous **St Stephen's Green** **E**. During the 18th century the square was almost completely surrounded by elegant town houses. Some survive today, though many conservationists despair at the rapidly declining number. Inside the square is a delightful park with flower gardens and an artificial lake favoured by waterfowl. Among many sculptures and monuments is a memorial to the poet and playwright W.B. Yeats by Henry Moore. Nearby is a bust to commemorate Yeats's friend, Countess Constance Markievicz, who defended the square during the 1916 insurrection, and who was the first woman elected to the British House of Commons (although she declined to take her seat, preferring the Dáil).

Another statue honours the man who paid for landscaping the square: Lord Ardilaun, son of the founder of the Guinness brewery. Some thirsty sightseers might be inspired to find a nearby pub and raise a toast to the stout-hearted benefactor.

Medieval Dublin

Dublin Castle **F** (Mon–Fri 10am–4.45pm, Sat and Sun 2–4.45pm; charge; www.dublincastle.ie) was begun in the 13th century, set on a hill above the original Viking settlement on the south bank of the River Liffey, but was mostly rebuilt during the 18th century. Over the years it has served as a seat of government, a prison, a courthouse, and occasionally as a fortress under siege. Many visiting heads of state have stayed in the lavish State Apartments.

Just behind the castle is the **Chester Beatty Library** **G** (Mon–Fri 10am–5pm, Sat 11am–5pm, Sun 1–5pm; closed Mon Oct–Apr; free; www.cbl.ie), a collection of priceless manuscripts and miniatures: jade books from China, early Arabic tomes on geography and astronomy, a sampling of Korans, and rare Gospel texts. Around the corner from the castle stands **City Hall**, built in the late 18th century in solid, classical style. Downstairs, an exhibition tells the story of the Irish capital.

Dublin has two noteworthy cathedrals, and although it is the official capital of what is a predominantly Catholic country, both belong to the Protestant Church of Ireland.

Christ Church Cathedral ⓗ (Mon–Fri 9.45am–6.15pm Sat 9.45am–4.15pm, Sun 12.30–2.30pm, 4.30–6.15pm in summer; Mon–Sat 9.45am–4.15pm, Sun 12.30–2.30pm in winter; charge; www.ccdub.ie) is the older of the two, dating from 1038. One unusual architectural touch is the covered pedestrian bridge over Winetavern Street, which links the church and its Synod Hall. This was built during the Victorian era, but doesn't spoil the overall mood. Otherwise, the cathedral contains Romanesque as well as Early English and fine neo-Gothic elements.

Christ Church Cathedral

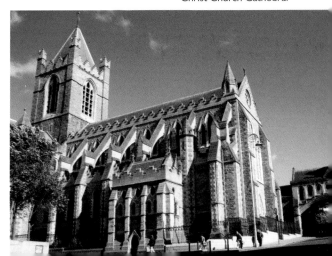

The Oliver St John Gogarty Bar in Temple Bar

The crypt, now displaying many of Christ Church's valuable treasures, runs under the length of the church, and is a surviving remnant from the 12th century, during which time the cathedral was expanded by Strongbow *(see page 16)*, whose remains lie buried here. Although regarded as authentic for many decades, modern scholars are in heated debate about the authenticity of the Strongbow tomb. You can see the fine statue of a recumbent cross-legged knight in full armour upstairs.

If you would like to delve more deeply into Irish history, you could visit the Synod Hall to see **Dublinia** and the Viking World (Apr–Sept daily 10am–4.15pm; Oct–Mar daily 10am–4pm; charge; www.dublinia.ie). This impressive multimedia heritage centre depicts how Dubliners lived in the medieval city, offering Viking artefacts and a closing audiovisual show.

A short walk south from Christ Church Cathedral leads to Dublin's newer and larger cathedral, **St Patrick's** ❶

(Mar–Oct Mon–Sat 9am–6pm, Sun 9–11am, 12.45–3pm, 4.15–6pm; Nov–Feb Mon–Sat 9am–5pm, Sun 9–4.30pm; charge; www.stpatrickscathedral.ie), which is dedicated to Ireland's national saint. It is said that St Patrick himself baptised 5th-century converts at a well on this very site; indeed, a stone slab used for covering the well can be found in the northwest of the cathedral. This church was consecrated in 1192, but the present structure dates mostly from the 13th and 14th centuries. The cathedral is known for its association with Jonathan Swift, author of *Gulliver's Travels*, who was appointed dean in 1713 and served until his death in 1745. Many Swiftian relics can be seen in a corner of the north transept, and a simple brass plate in the floor near the entrance marks his grave. Next to this you can see the tomb of the mysterious Stella, one of the two great loves of his life. Above the lintel of the robing room you can read his own bitter epitaph, written in Latin: 'Savage indignation can no

Temple Bar

Temple Bar is a network of small streets full of studios, galleries, second-hand bookshops, clothing outlets and music stores. There are countless restaurants, pubs and crafts shops. Many Dubliners regard it as a tourist trap, but it has some worthwhile cultural centres.

Project Arts Centre: displays avant-garde painting and sculpture.

The Button Factory: workshop and venue for concerts.

Irish Film Institute: arthouse cinema with bookshop, café/restaurant, bar and film archive.

Gallery of Photography: exhibits Irish and international work.

National Photographic Archive: maintains and exhibits historical images of Ireland.

DESIGNyard: displays and sells Irish jewellery, art and furniture.

The Ark: a cultural centre for children.

The Four Courts

longer gnaw his heart. Go, traveller, and imitate, if you can, this earnest and dedicated defender of liberty'.

The talented choirboys of St Patrick's Cathedral sing at the services given every day of the week except Saturdays. A joint choir formed from both cathedrals was the first to sing Handel's *Messiah* when the composer was in Dublin in 1742. A copy from the year 1799 can be seen in **Marsh's Library** ❶ (Mon, Wed–Fri 10am–1pm and 2–5pm, Sat 10.30am–1pm; charge; www.marshlibrary.ie), Ireland's first public library, founded in 1701.

Called the 'Left Bank' by tourist officials, **Temple Bar** ❶ (*see page 33*) is Dublin's cultural quarter, running from Westmoreland Street to Christ Church Cathedral. With its 18th- and 19th-century architecture it's not just the cultural quarter of Dublin, but also a land of themed bars and raucous nightclubs. It's at its best on Saturday morning in Cow's Lane when there is a market selling vintage clothing, crafts and high fashion by hip young designers.

The North Bank

The most impressive building located on the north bank of the Liffey is the domed home of the **Four Courts** (originally the Chancery, Common Pleas, Exchequer and King's Bench).

This is the magnificent work of James Gandon, the respected 18th-century English-born architect who also designed Dublin's Custom House. The courthouse was seriously damaged by prolonged shelling during the 1922 civil war. After lengthy reconstruction, however, it was restored, and justice continues to be dispensed in the Four Courts.

St Michan's Church (Mar–Oct Mon–Fri 10am–12.45pm and 2–4.45pm, Sat 10am–12.45pm; Nov–Mar Mon–Fri 12.30–3.30pm, Sat 10am–12.45pm; charge for tours of the crypt) just around the corner in Church Street, was founded in 1095 but has been rebuilt several times. Among the curiosities is an unusual 'Penitent's Pew', in which sinners had to sit and confess their sins aloud to the whole congregation. In the crypt, wood coffins and mummies can be seen in a remarkable state of preservation. Some of them have been here for about 800 years, saved from deterioration by the dry atmosphere. You can touch the finger of the mummified crusader for good luck.

The last imposing official building to be designed by the architect James Gandon was the **King's Inns** ⬤, which houses the headquarters of the Irish legal profession. It contains an important law library and a magnificent dining hall, where grand portraits of many judges decorate the walls.

On the north side of Parnell Square is Charlemont House, an attractive 18th-century mansion which is now the **Dublin City Gallery The Hugh Lane** ⬤ (Tue–Thur 10am–6pm, Fri–Sat 10am–5pm, Sun 11am–5pm; free; www.hughlane.ie). It includes works from the fine collection of Sir Hugh Lane, whose drowning in the *Lusitania* disaster of 1915 (see page 59) provoked a long legal battle over custody of his paintings. The current agreement assures the Dublin City Gallery three-quarters of the contested legacy, including works by Corot, Courbet, Manet, Monet and Rousseau. The gallery also houses the Francis Bacon Studio (charge),

Evening in Phoenix Park

its contents transported from London in 1998 and meticulously recreated, along with displays of the famous artist's works.

Next door to the gallery, **The Dublin Writers Museum** (Mon–Sat 10am–5pm, Sun 11am–5pm; charge; www.writers museum.com) displays photographs, manuscripts and first editions relating to writers such as Swift, Shaw, Yeats, O'Casey, Joyce, Beckett and Behan. At 35 North Great George's Street is the **James Joyce Centre** (Tue–Sat 10am–5pm, Sun noon–5pm; charge; www.jamesjoyce.ie) for Joyce enthusiasts.

Beyond the Centre

Phoenix Park provides Dubliners with nearly 8 sq km (3 sq miles) of beautiful parkland. Its huge monument is an obelisk honouring the Duke of Wellington, who was born in Ireland but played down his Irishness, quipping that although a man may be born in a stable, that wouldn't make him a horse. Among the buildings discreetly located in the park are the residence of the President of Ireland (*Áras an Uachtaráin*), Farmleigh House, an Edwardian stately house and garden (www.farmleigh.ie), and the Ashtown Castle Heritage Centre, which details the history of the park and its flora and fauna. On the northeast side of the park, Dublin **Zoo** provides education and diversion; it is noted for breeding lion cubs in captivity.

In Kilmainham, a stone tower gate guards the grounds of the **Royal Hospital**, which was a home for army pensioners.

Now it is the **Irish Museum of Modern Art** (Tue–Sat 10am–5.30pm, from 10.30am Wed, Sun noon–5.30pm; free; www.imma.ie) and holds first-class temporary exhibitions.

The forbidding **Kilmainham Gaol** (Apr–Sept daily 9.30am–5pm; Oct–Mar Mon–Sat 9.30am–4pm, Sun 10am–5pm; charge; www.heritageireland.ie) has been carefully restored. Many heroes of Irish nationalism lived and died as prisoners here. The central cellblock shows exhibits from Ireland's stormy history.

Many make their way to the city's biggest commercial enterprise, the **Guinness Brewery**, situated at St James' Gate since 1759. Its dark, full-bodied stout is world-renowned. Visitors to its award-winning **Storehouse** (daily 9.30am–5pm, until 7pm July–Aug; www.guinness-storehouse.com) get an entertaining explanation of how the brew is made and a sample of the finished product.

Malahide Castle

DUBLIN DAYTRIPS

North of Dublin

In the northeastern part of the Bay, **Howth peninsula** makes an appealing starting point for those wishing to venture out of Dublin. From the vantage point of the 170-m (560-ft) Hill of Howth, you can survey the bay and the sea. Howth Harbour, on the north side of the peninsula, is a fishing port and haven for pleasure boats. From here you can see and visit Ireland's Eye, an islet 1.5km (1 mile) offshore that is popular with birds and bird-watchers.

Malahide, a small resort town, is best known for its **castle**

An early Christian high cross at Monasterboice

(Apr–Sept Mon–Sat 10am–5pm, Sun 10am–6pm; Oct–Mar Mon–Sat 10am–5pm, Sun 11am–12.45pm and 2–5pm; charge; www.malahidecastle.com), a two-turreted medieval pile. The spirit of the Talbot family, who resided here for 791 years, still pervades, and is explained by an interpretive centre. Part of the National Portrait Collection is housed here and the castle's rooms are fully furnished, and include a medieval great hall. The Talbot Botanic Gardens were started in 1948, and contain 5,000 labelled species on 250 acres, and seven glasshouses. It is the most important botanic collection after London's Kew Gardens.

Drogheda ❷, a small industrial town, straddles the River Boyne near the site of the 1690 battle in which King James II failed to recover the English crown *(see page 19)*. This medieval city was surrounded by a wall with 10 gates – you can still drive through the 13th-century **St Lawrence's Gate**, with its two towers. In the town centre **St Peter's Church** has been dedicated to St Oliver Plunkett (1628–81), the Archbishop of Armagh who was executed by the British for an alleged papist plot. Several relics of the local saint are displayed in the church, including the actual door of his cell at Newgate Prison and, most amazing of all, his head, which is embalmed and kept in a gold case in a side altar.

About 10km (6 miles) to the northwest is **Monasterboice** (St Buite's Abbey), one of Ireland's numerous ancient monastic settlements. Over it stands the jagged top of what is thought to have been the tallest round tower in Ireland, 34m (110ft) high. Along with the remains of two ruined churches there are three important examples of early Christian high crosses, with intricately carved figures.

A high medieval gatehouse guards the approach to **Old Mellifont Abbey** (May–Sept daily 10am–6pm; charge; www.heritageireland.ie), Ireland's most important early Cistercian monastery. Among the buildings stand the remains of a large church and the Lavabo, a graceful octagonal building of which only four sides remain. The abbey is set in peaceful and verdant country.

Winter lottery

The overwhelming demand to see Newgrange during the winter solstice has forced Irish Heritage to hold a lottery. Visitors can sign up in the welcome centre. Or you can email your postal address and contact phone number to brunaboinne@opw.ie and they'll enter your name. From an average 35,000 entries, 50 names are chosen.

The sacred mound at Newgrange

Newgrange ❸ (Brú na Boinne Visitor Centre; Mar–Apr and Oct daily 9.30am–5.30pm; May and late-Sept 9am–6.30pm; June–early Sept 9am–7pm; Nov–Feb 9.30am–5pm; charge; www.heritageireland.ie), a large Neolithic tomb in the Boyne Valley, looks like a man-made hilltop, but is in fact an amazing feat of prehistoric engineering – one of Europe's best examples of a passage-grave. The narrow tunnel leading to the central shrine is positioned to let the sun shine in on the shortest day of the year, 21 December. The 19-m (62-ft) tunnel is just high and wide enough to walk through at a crouch. At its end you can stand in the circular vault and look up at the ceiling to see the remarkable 4,000-year-old technique used in its construction.

Carvings in spiral, circular and diamond designs decorate the stones in the inner sanctum and entrance. Outside, a dozen large, upright stones, about a third the original number, form a protective circle. Access is by guided tour only; numbers are limited, so arrive early (last tours 90 min before closing). There are two more Neolithic tumuli at Knowth and Dowth.

The scribes and artists of the monastery at **Kells** in County Meath, produced the nation's most beautiful book, now on display at Trinity College in Dublin (*see page 27*). The town of Kells has grown up around the monastic settlement, and there is a fine Celtic cross standing at the main traffic junction. In the churchyard are several other stone crosses and a 30-m (100-ft) high round tower.

As its name indicates, **Trim ❹** is a well-kept, tidy town, but the English name is derived from the Irish *Baile Atha Trium*, which means 'the town of the Elder Tree Ford'. Trim claims it has Ireland's largest medieval **castle** (Nov–Jan Sat–Sun 10am–5pm; Apr–Oct daily 10am–6pm; charge; www.heritageireland.ie), once a Norman stronghold. Vast it is, but time has left only the bare bones. The Dublin Gate in the south once contained a prison. Across the river, the Yellow Steeple was part of an Augustinian abbey established in the 13th century; the tower was blown up to keep it out of Cromwell's hands.

West of Dublin

County Kildare has some of the greenest pastures in all of Ireland. It's a great area for sports, and there are plenty of historic sites amid the rolling hills. **Maynooth**, a pleasant town with an historic college and the ruins of a 12th-century castle, was famed in the 19th and 20th century as a training centre for priests. Founded in 1795, **St Patrick's College** was one of the foremost Catholic

Ruined monastery

The ruins of an ancient monastery are at the southern end of County Kildare, in the village of Castledermot. Two beautifully carved crosses remain near the portal of a church that could be as much as 1,000 years old. The design of this ruin is repeated in a new church just a few yards behind it.

seminaries in the world. It is now part of the National University of Ireland.

On the edge of Celbridge village, **Castletown House** ❺ (guided tours only, mid-Mar–mid-Nov Wed–Sat 10am–5pm, Sun 10–6pm; charge; www.castletownhouse.ie) stands at the end of a long avenue of trees. This vast stately home, in Palladian style, was erected in 1722 for the speaker of the Irish House of Commons, William Conolly, and has been restored and refurnished with 18th-century antiques and paintings. Conolly's widow ordered the construction of a monstrous obelisk 5km (3 miles) from the house. Known as Conolly's Folly, it was erected to provide jobs for local workers suffering from the Great Famine of the 1740s.

The administrative centre of the county, **Naas** (the Irish *Nas na Riogh*, means 'Assembly Place of the Kings') has an important racecourse. So does nearby Punchestown, but the capital of horse racing and breeding is the **Curragh** ❻, a 2,000 hectare stretch of flat racing turf, grazed by sheep and used for exercise gallops by many training stables. It's a shock to come upon a modern grandstand – site of the Irish Sweeps Derby – in the middle of this vast plain.

Many winners of the biggest races are born near Kildare Town at the **National Stud Farm** (daily mid-Feb–mid-Nov 9.30am–5pm; mid-Nov–mid-Dec 9.30am–5pm; charge; www.irishnationalstud.ie). Here thoroughbreds live in a first-class 'horse resort'. Beside the Irish Horse Museum, there is an immaculate **Japanese Garden** – once a bog, now a world of tidy shrubs and trees. There's even a lotus pond, teahouse and red wooden bridge.

The town of **Kildare** is also remembered for the double monastery (monks and nuns) founded there by 5th-century St Brigid. Though Vikings and other invaders damaged the buildings quite badly, the shape of the 19th-century **cathedral** features 13th-century elements. Nearby you can inspect an ancient round tower still in very good shape, with stairs all the way to the summit.

South of Dublin

Dún Laoghaire ❼ (pronounced Dunleary), just south of Dublin, is Ireland's leading yachting centre and a car ferry terminal. The piers at the harbour are 2km (1 mile) long, leaving plenty of space between for the huge fleet of pleasure boats that dock here. Construction of the harbour was a great feat of 19th-century engineering – and is still impressive.

Around 1.5km (1 mile) south at **Sandycove** is an 18th-century tower. James Joyce lived in it, and used this experience in the opening of *Ulysses*. The Martello Tower (named after a Corsican headland with a fort) was part of the coastal defences built to keep Napoleon at bay. It has been turned into a museum dedicated to Joyce, the **James Joyce Tower and Museum** (Apr–Sept Mon–Sat 10am–1pm and 2–5pm, Sun 2–6pm; charge; Oct–Mar open to groups of 20 plus by appointment; tel: 01-280 9265; www.visitdublin.com). A second Martello Tower can be seen on Dalkey Island, the largest of a group of islands off Dalkey.

Powerscourt Waterfall

Just across the border in County Wicklow, the popular resort of **Bray** has a 2-km (1-mile) sand-and-shingle beach backed by an esplanade. The coast here is mostly sandy and low-lying, and the county's interior is known as the Garden of Ireland.

West of Bray, near Enniskerry, is the grand estate

of **Powerscourt** ❽ (daily 9.30am–5.30pm or dusk in winter; charge; www.powerscourt.ie). Covering 20 hectares (47 acres) of glorious countryside and gardens, the estate has an 18th-century, 100-room mansion at its centre, which was damaged in a fire in 1974. Today it contains an exhibition devoted to the history of the estate. From the house, disciplined terraces descend to a lake with a fountain in the middle. The garden centre is also worth a visit, as is the Powerscourt Waterfall, 5km (3 miles) south of the house.

In a narrow, wooded valley with two lakes stand the evocative ruins of the ancient monastic settlement of **Glendalough** ❾ (mid-Mar–mid-Oct 9.30am–6pm; mid-Oct–mid-Mar 9.30am–5pm; free; www.glendalough.ie). The hermit St Kevin founded the monastery here in the 6th century, evidently inspired by the breathtaking, remote scenery. He planned it as a small, contemplative institution, but as its fame spread far and wide, Glendalough of the Seven Churches became an important monastic centre, until 1398, when it was destroyed by Anglo-Normans.

The buildings which survive date from the 8th and 12th centuries. The most famous is the **round tower**, which is 34m (112ft) high and 16m (52ft) in circumference at the base. This was the place to sit out any sieges; its doorway

The Wicklow Way

You'll need the better part of a week to see all of this ancient path, which stretches 132km (82 miles) from the suburbs of Dublin to the Wexford border town of Clonegal. A shorter option is the popular stretch from Knockree, 5km (3 miles) west of Enniskerry, to Glendalough. It'll take you about three days to cover this area, and you'll be able to step foot on the highest point of the trail – White Hill, from which on a clear day you can see the mountains in Wales.

is built 3.5m (11ft) above the ground – enough to discourage even Vikings from invading. Remnants of a cathedral, stone churches and decorated crosses can also be seen, and the original gateway to the settlement, the only one of its kind in Ireland, is still standing. Inside, on the right, a cross-inscribed stone may have marked the limit of the sanctuary granted to those who took refuge within the monastery. In the graveyard, tombstones dating back hundreds of years sit next to more recent graves.

In **Avondale,** you can visit **Avondale House and Gardens** (house, mid-Mar–late Oct daily 11am–6pm; charge; park, daily to dusk), the home of Charles Stewart Parnell, the great 19th-century Irish leader, which has been restored in 1850s style. It is set in an area of verdant forest and woodland and makes an ideal destination for walkers. The grand **Russborough House** (Apr and Oct Sun and holidays 10am–5.30pm; May–Sept daily 10am–6pm; charge; www.russborough.ie), near Blessington, is an 18th-century manor in Palladian style. Today it houses the Sir Alfred Beit Art Collection, and is beautifully and richly decorated, offering magnificent views across the ornamental lake towards the splendid Wicklow mountains.

In the Irish National Heritage Park

Mudflat harbour

In the 9th century Wexford was called *Waesfjord*, meaning 'the harbour of the mudflats'. At low tide, when the bay empties like a sink, the original name still seems appropriate.

THE SOUTHEAST

Over the whole year, the southeast enjoys up to an hour more sunshine a day than other parts of Ireland. The better to see – and enjoy – the varied mountains and pastures, rivers, beautiful beaches and delightful old towns.

Enniscorthy (the Irish *Inis Coirthe* means Rock Island) is a colourful inland port on the River Slaney, navigable from here to Wexford. High above the steep streets of the town, Vinegar Hill is a good vantage point for viewing the countryside. It was the scene of the last battle of the 1798 Rising, during which British General Lake overwhelmed the Wexford rebels armed with pitchforks and pikes. **Enniscorthy Castle** (Mon–Fri 9–5pm, Sat–Sun noon–5pm; charge; www.enniscorthycastle. ie), in the centre of town, is an imposing Norman keep, rebuilt during the 16th century. It reopened in 2011 after a major renovation, and is benefitting from its resemblance to Harry Potter's school, Hogwarts.

Wexford

Wexford, the county seat, 24km (15 miles) south of Enniscorthy, was one of the first Viking settlements. A few ancient monuments survive and are well signposted, with informative plaques explaining local legends.

The **Irish National Heritage Park** ❿ (daily 9.30am–6.30pm, until 5.30pm in winter; charge; www.inhp.com) in Ferrycarrig, north of town, contains a collection of life-size replicas of ancient dwellings, burial sites, old monastic settlements and fortifications, from early Irish man to the 12th century. Reminders of the area's seafaring past are on view at the

Maritime Museum, housed in an old lightship, moored permanently in the harbour of the picturesque village of Kilmore Quay, about 25km (15 miles) south of Wexford.

In October, the Wexford Opera Festival attracts world performers and fans for little-known works. Southeast of the town, the resort of **Rosslare** has a 10-km (6-mile) crescent of beach. At Rosslare Harbour, car ferries arrive from and depart for Fishguard, Pembroke Dock, Roscoff and Cherbourg.

The tip of the **Hook peninsula** has a tall, 700-year-old lighthouse that warns mariners of treacherous rocks and signals the entrance to Waterford harbour. A light has been kept burning at Hook Head for the past 1,500 years.

The Norse established ports such as Dublin and Wexford, but it somehow never occurred to them to found permanent settlements inland. It was the Normans who moved 32km (20 miles) up the estuary to build the town of **New Ross** ⑪, still an important inland port. By the riverbank you will see the tall masts of the Dunbrody Famine Ship (daily 9–6pm, Oct–Mar 5pm; charge; www. dunbrody.com), a full scale replica of a sailing ship built in 1845 to transport emigrants to north America.

The isolated hamlet of **Dunganstown**, near New Ross, was the birthplace of US President John F. Kennedy's great grandfather.

Waterford crystal in the making

A plaque marks the cottage from which he emigrated to Boston. The assassinated president was much admired in Ireland and a group of Irish-Americans and the Irish government later created the **John F. Kennedy Arboretum**, above Dunganstown.

Waterford

Waterford ⑫ is a largely Georgian port 29km (18 miles) from the open sea. From the far side of the River Suir, its long quayside presents a pretty image. Founded in the 9th century, the town did not gain a charter until 1205, granted by King John. The heritage centre has ancient relics from the Norse and Norman settlements and audiovisual displays. Municipal mementos, including Waterford's important collection of medieval charters, are preserved inside **Reginald's Tower**, the city's most venerable building (June–Sept daily 10am–6pm; Easter–May and Oct daily 10am–5pm; Nov–Easter Wed–Sun 10am–5pm; charge). The walls of this giant circular fortification, 3m (10ft) thick and about 24m (80ft) tall, have survived many sieges since being erected in 1003.

Among other attractions are the Garter Lane Arts Centre, a lively venue in a converted town house; the Mall, an elegant Georgian street beginning at the Quay; and Waterford City Hall, built in the 1780s, which has many fine features, including two small theatres and a Council Chamber illuminated by a splendid chandelier made from **Waterford crystal**.

The golden age of Waterford crystal ran from 1783 to 1851. After a century's lapse, production resumed, only to cease again in 2009. The skills of lowing and cutting lead crystal continue to be demonstrated in the **Waterford Crystal Visitor Centre** on the Mall (factory tour Jan–Feb Mon–Sat 9am–3.15pm; Mar Mon–Sat 9am–3.15pm, Sun 9.30am–3.15pm; Apr–Oct Mon–Sat 9am–4.15pm, Sun 9.30am–4.15pm; Nov–Dec Mon–Fri 9.30am–3.15pm; charge; www.waterfordvisitor centre.com).

In **Lismore** ⑬ at the western edge of the county, the **Lismore Experience**, another educational multimedia show, tells the history of this small town founded in the 7th century by St Carthage. Also, **Ormond Castle** in Carrick-on-Suir is a fine example of an old Elizabethan manor, now restored to its 16th-century glory.

Counties **Kilkenny** and **Tipperary** both feature stunning scenery and imposing ruins. Tipperary was home of the kings of Munster; Kilkenny entered history as the ancient Kingdom of Ossory. The main town in County Tipperary is **Clonmel**, where parts of the 14th-century walls can still be seen. The turreted West Gate was rebuilt in 1831 on the site of an original gate. The county museum in Parnell Street is well worth a visit.

The name of the town of **Cahir** is a short version of the Irish for 'Fortress of the Dun Abounding in Fish'. Its setting, on the River Suir, is both attractive and strategic. A seemingly

Cahir Castle

The Rock of Cashel

impregnable **castle** (daily Apr–mid-June 9.30am–5.30pm; mid-June–mid-Sept 9am–7pm; mid-Sept–Mar 9.30am–4.30pm; charge; www.heritageireland.ie) guards the crucial crossing. Built on the river's lovely islet – a site fortified since the 3rd century – the present castle dates from the 15th century. It's in a fine state of restoration, and guided tours point out military details, such as musket slits, a portcullis and a cannonball embedded high in one of the walls. While you're in Cahir, take a look at **Swiss Cottage** (mid-Apr–mid-Oct daily 10–6pm; charge; www.heritageireland.ie), an early 19th-century romantic cottage, in the bright Regency style. It has been fully restored right down to the thatched roof and original French wallpaper.

Cashel

In **Cashel** ⑭ (County Tipperary), monastic runs crown an imposing hilltop. The **Rock of Cashel** (daily mid-Mar–mid-June 9am–5.30pm; mid-June–mid-Sept 9am–7pm; mid-Sept–mid-Oct 9am–5.30pm; mid-Oct–mid-Mar 9am–4.30pm; charge; www.heritageireland.ie), is a 61-m (200-ft) high outcrop of limestone, where the kings of Munster had their headquarters from the 4th to the 12th centuries. St Patrick visited in 450 and baptised King Aengus and his brothers. In 1101 ecclesiastical authorities built an Irish-Romanesque church on it. **Cormac's Chapel** (consecrated in 1134) is unique in that it was built by Irish monks who interpreted architectural styles they had studied in Europe. It features a steeply pitched stone roof, rows of blank arches and two oddly positioned towers. Stone-carvings of beasts and abstract designs decorate the doorway and arches.

The chapel is dwarfed by the **cathedral** which abuts it. This structure, dating from the 13th century, has thick and well-preserved walls, but the roof collapsed during the 18th century. On the positive side, the resulting hole lets the sunlight stream in, helping to clarify the many architectural details, as well as the exquisite medieval stone-carvings.

Inside the entrance, St Patrick's Cross is one of the oldest crosses in Ireland, and it looks like it – the sculptures on both sides are very weather-beaten. The cross rises up from the 'Coronation Stone', said to have been a pagan sacrificial altar.

It was in the lively market town of **Thurles**, in 1174, that the Irish forces defeated the Anglo-Norman army led by Strongbow (*see page 16*). Seven hundred years later, the town was to be

Holy Cross Abbey

Local life in Kilkenny

the birthplace of the Gaelic Athletic Association (GAA), now an amateur sports organisation. The GAA centre offers a multimedia show on the history of Gaelic games. The most conspicuous landmark of the town, the Catholic Cathedral, was built in a 19th-century version of the Romanesque style. The square bell tower, 38m (125ft) high, can be seen for miles around.

On the west bank of the River Suir, 6km (4 miles) south of Thurles is the Cistercian **Holy Cross Abbey**. Construction of the church here, which is still in use, started in Romanesque style, but slowly evolved into Gothic. The solid white walls, enhanced by window-tracery, reach up to a perfectly restored 15th-century ceiling. A triple-arched recess contains seats of honour carved from jet-black marble and decorated with ancient coats of arms. Another detail is the night stairs, down which the monks stumbled from their sleeping quarters at 2am to chant matins. One of the bells in the tower was cast in the early 13th century, making it Ireland's oldest.

Kilkenny

Kilkenny ⓫ has a colourful past and present. Among other surprises, you will find, smack in the city centre, an enormous medieval castle with acres of lawns – and a river to boot. This was the capital of the old Kingdom of Ossory, a small, feuding realm in pre-Norman Ireland.

Parliament, which convened here in 1366, passed the notorious but ineffectual Statutes of Kilkenny, with the aim of segregating the Irish from the Anglo-Normans; in those days intermarriage was seen as high treason. In the 17th century an independent Irish parliament met here for several years. Oliver Cromwell took the town for the English in 1650, suffering heavy losses in the process.

The Irish *Cill Choinnigh* means St Canice's church. **St Canice's Cathedral**, built in the 13th century, is on the original site of the church which gave the town its name. Though Cromwell's rampaging troops badly damaged the building, it has since been restored to an admirable state. Alongside it is a round tower.

Kilkenny Castle (daily Apr–May 10.30am–5pm; June–Aug 9.30am–7pm; Sept 10am–6.30pm; Oct–Mar 10.30am–12.45pm; charge; www.kilkennycastle.ie) was built in the 13th century to replace the primitive fortress erected by Strongbow. The Butler family, one of the great Anglo-Norman dynasties, held the castle until 1935, but today it is owned by the Irish state. Its ornate Georgian stable houses the headquarters of the Irish Crafts Council, a gallery and the Kilkenny Craft Shop. Kilkenny was at the forefront of the revival of traditional handicrafts and innovative design in Ireland, and the 'craft trail' (brochures available locally; www.madeinkilkenny.ie) is well worth following.

Kilkenny Castle

Kilkenny is packed with bright shops. In the High Street, the Tholsel (city hall), dating from the 18th century, has an eight-sided clock tower. **Rothe House**, a Tudor town house dating from 1594, has been restored as a museum. The exhibits range from Stone Age tools unearthed locally to medieval relics.

Near **Thomastown** you can visit the partially restored ruins of the Cistercian **Jerpoint Abbey** (daily Mar and mid-Sept 9am–5.30pm; Oct 9am–5pm; Nov–early Dec 9.30am–4pm; charge; www.heritageireland.ie). Founded in the mid-12th century by the King of Ossory, it had a brief, troubled history before succumbing to the dissolution of the monasteries in 1540. Parts of it retain their Romanesque lines, but the square central tower with its stepped battlements was added during the 15th century. Much of the sculptural work in the cloister and church is intact, and you can see larger-than-life carvings of knights and saints, which are inspiring monuments both to those they honour, and to the talented and devoted sculptors who worked here in the Middle Ages.

St Finbarr's Cathedral in Cork City

THE SOUTHWEST

Cork

Ireland's largest county marries gently rolling farmland with rugged, stony peninsulas and delightful bays. Enclosed by steep hills, **Cork City** ⑯ has all the facilities of an important commercial and industrial centre, but its

atmosphere is unique. The
River Lee divides into two
channels to the west of the
city centre, leaving the centre on an island connected
to its north and south banks
by numerous bridges, with
seagulls flying overhead and
swans gliding by.

Inside St Finbarr's Cathedral

The city's name is an
anglicisation of *Corcaigh*,
or 'Marshy Place', which is
how the area looked in the
6th century when St Finbarr arrived to found a church and
school. In the year 820 the Vikings raided marshy Cork,
destroying the institutions and houses. They liked the lay of
the land and returned to build their own town on the same
site. This destruction and rebuilding was repeated like a pat-
tern in the 17th century and then again during the 'Troubles'
of 1919–21.

The main office for Cork and Kerry Tourism is located
on the Grand Parade in Cork and offers free maps of the
city centre. Cork's beauty begs slow exploration and one can
easily spend the day strolling along its narrow canals and
winding streets.

Patrick Street, the wide main street of Cork, is curved
because it was built above a river channel. It makes for great
window-shopping anytime and is full of people promenad-
ing on Saturday afternoons. A venture across the south
channel of the River Lee will take you to **St Finbarr's
Cathedral**. The latest version was built in the 19th century
and follows the lofty French-Gothic style, with arches upon
arches. Across the river's north channel on the Christy Ring
Bridge and up the hill is Shandon Church. This distinctive

steeple has always been a favourite city landmark. Visitors can climb up through the clockwork intricacies and even play a tune on the bells.

Nearby, at Sunday's Well you can visit the fully restored 19th/early 20th-century cells of the **Cork City Gaol**. The same building high above the city was the location of Cork's first radio station which is now a delightfully idiosyncratic radio museum.

County Cork

Cork is a good centre for excursions. **Blarney Castle** **⑰** (Mon–Sat, May 9am–6.30pm; June–Aug 9am–7pm; Sept 9am–6.30pm; Oct–Apr 9am–sunset or 6pm; Sun summer 9.30am–5.30pm, winter 9.30am–sunset; charge; www.blarneycastle.ie) is 8km (5 miles) to the west. The original owner of the castle, chieftain Cormac MacCarthy, had a habit of employing

Cobh Harbour

soothing but evasive chatter (dubbed the 'blarney') as delaying tactics. Today, in order to acquire similar eloquence, tourists climb up to the battlement, lie flat on their backs, hang on to two iron bars and extend the head backwards in order to kiss an awkwardly placed stone. Most visitors play along with this preposterous legend.

The castle itself is worth a visit, even if mighty hordes of tourists do besiege it every summer. The formidable keep was built in the middle of the 15th century, while the private park, in which the castle stands, includes a grove of ancient yew trees, said to be a site of Druid worship.

Cobh ⑱, the seaport of Cork city, lies about 24km (15 miles) east of Cork City. It is pronounced 'Cove', which is exactly what it means in Irish.

From Queen Victoria's visit in 1849, until 1922, Cobh was called Queenstown. The port is touched by nostalgia – from the days of the great transatlantic liners and the earlier, more tragic traffic of desperate emigrants fleeing the Irish famine for Canada or America. **The Queenstown Story** provides a particular insight into this era. The Cunard shipping office is now a bank. High above the harbour, the spire of the **Cathedral of St Colman** reaches heavenward. Recitals are given in the summer on the cathedral's 47-bell carillon.

In Midleton, to the northeast of Cobh, visit the **Old Midleton Distillery** (guided tours Mar–Oct daily 10am–6pm, last tour at 5pm; Nov–Feb daily at 11.30am, 2.30pm and 4pm; charge; www.tours.jamesonwhiskey.com) in a converted whiskey distillery that dates back to the late 18th century. It tells the story of Irish whiskey via an audiovisual presentation, and offers a tour with tastings.

The town of **Youghal** (in English pronounced 'Yawl'), east of Midleton, is a resort with 8km (5 miles) of beach and a long seafaring history. The town walls from the Middle Ages can still be seen.

On the site of the main town gate is the **clock tower** from 1776. The high street runs right through it with the structure's four narrow floors and belfry rising above an arched platform over the street. The attractive tower was once a prison, and insurrectionists were hanged from the windows to set an example to the populace.

The most impressive monument in Youghal, **St Mary's Collegiate Church** (Church of Ireland), is thought to have been founded in the 5th century. The present building dates largely from the 13th century, and was restored in the 19th. Among the monuments and tombs in the church is one built, in his own honour, by Richard Boyle, an Elizabethan adventurer and the first Earl of Cork. Myrtle Grove, a 16th-century house near the churchyard entrance, was briefly home to Sir Walter Raleigh. The Heritage Centre (www.eastcorktourism.com) on the quayside runs frequent guided tours.

The Old Head of Kinsale

Steep green hills shelter the seaport of **Kinsale** ⑲, about 29km (18 miles) south of Cork. Its wide, sheltered harbour is a joy to sailors and sightseers alike. Kinsale is renowned for its restaurants, which are among the best in southwest Ireland.

Kinsale besieged

Kinsale was under siege in 1601 as Spanish troops, who had sailed to aid the Irish against Queen Elizabeth, were defeated, sparking the 'flight of the Earls' (the exodus of the Irish nobility) and the redistribution of their lands.

Today, the **harbour** is used by fishing boats, dinghies and yachts. Ashore are fortifications including the classic star-shaped **Charles Fort** (daily Nov–mid-Mar 10am–5pm; mid-Mar–Oct 10am–6pm; charge; www.heritageireland. ie), the Norman church of St Multose, a museum housing Edward III's first town charter, and the **Desmond Castle International Museum of Wine**.

Migratory birds inhabit the **Old Head** of Kinsale, 16km (10 miles) beyond the town. A modern lighthouse here is the successor to a beacon dating back to pre-Christian times. It was off the Old Head that a German submarine torpedoed the world-famous liner, the *Lusitania*, on 7 May 1915, resulting in the loss of 1,500 lives. The inquest into the disaster was held in the Kinsale Court House.

Clonakilty, between Kinsale and Bantry, is home to the **West Cork Model Railway Village** (daily 11am–5pm; July–Aug from 10am; charge) that depicts the area's six towns, with a working model of the defunct West Cork Railway.

The town of **Bantry** nestles between steep green hills and a tranquil bay. The main sight is Bantry House (Mar–Oct daily 10am–6pm; charge; www.bantryhouse.ie), a part-Georgian, part-Victorian stately home full of tapestries, paintings and furnishing and set in sub-tropical gardens.

Heading counter-clockwise around the bay from Bantry, the highway weaves through more rocky hills until it descends upon **Glengarriff** ⑳, where the beauty of the setting and the pleasant climate account for its year-round popularity.

Boat trips touted by traditional boatmen in Glengarriff cruise past Seal Island, and you can opt to land on **Garinish Island** (Apr–Oct Mon–Sat 9.30am–dusk, Sun 11am–dusk; charge; www.heritageirealnd.ie) a 15-hectare (37-acre) garden. The flora comes from five continents, and the centrepiece is a walled **Italian garden**, surrounding a pool, with the gentle air of a paradisiacal perfume factory. Until 1910, Garinish was a bleak military outpost. From the top of the Martello tower, sentries once kept a lookout for Napoleonic invasion fleets; today, you can survey the luxuriant hills around the bay.

County Kerry

By any standard this is a spectacular part of the world: the Atlantic in all its moods, lakes designed for lovers or poets, and steep, evergreen mountains. **Killarney** ㉑ is a good base from which to explore the area. Seeing the sights here can be accomplished in many ways – by car, coach, bicycle, boat or even by 'jaunting car' – a horse-drawn rig driven by a *jarvey* (guide) who knows the territory and how to tell a story.

Due to logistical problems, it is best to visit the **Gap of Dunloe** on a fully organised excursion, usually a half-day trip. The Gap, a wild gorge 6km (4 miles) long, can be traversed on a pony, in a pony trap or on foot. Sound effects underline the weirdness of the eerie rock-strewn scenery as echoes bounce off the mountains – **MacGillycuddy's Reeks** in the west (the highest range in Ireland), and to the east, **Purple Mountain**. The long trek leads to the shore of the Upper Lake, where the tour continues by boat to Ross Castle. The scenery around the lakes – thick forests, stark crags and enchanted islands – could not be more romantic, but there's adventure, too: the **rapids** at Old Weir Bridge.

Muckross Abbey is a friary dating from the 15th century with a massive square tower, a cloister with Gothic arches on two sides, Norman or Romanesque on the others and an old, weathered yew tree. **Muckross House** (daily 9am–5.30pm, until 6pm July and Aug; charge; www.muckross-house.ie), which contains exhibits of Kerry crafts and folklore, is surrounded by outstanding gardens. Muckross Traditional Farms (same hours and website) is an enjoyable outdoor attraction recreating traditional farming methods and way of life in the 1930s.

Ring of Kerry

The **Ring of Kerry** ㉒ may well be the most sensational 180km (112 miles) you have ever driven. The ring is a circular route around a coast of rugged cliffs and the enthralling seascapes. This round-trip can be made in either direction, but here we proceed clockwise. Set aside a whole day.

The Ring of Kerry

Leaving Killarney, the road goes past lush lakeland. **Kenmare** is famous for lacemaking and the fish which fill its estuary. North of the small resort of Castlecove, 3km (2 miles) off the main road, are the ruins of **Staigue Fort**. A 2,500-year-old stronghold and one of Ireland's main archaeological wonders, this almost circular structure measures about 27m (90ft) across with a 6m (18ft) wall.

Near Caherdaniel, **Derrynane House**, the home of Daniel O'Connell (see page 20), has been fully restored and is now a museum (Apr and Oct Tue–Sun 1–5pm; May–Sept Mon–Sat 9am–6pm and Sun 11am–7pm; Nov–Mar Sat–Sun 1–5pm; charge; www.heritageireland.ie). Game fishing lures visitors to Waterville, as well as the scenery nearby: stark grey glaciated mountains on one side of the road, green fields and the sea on the other.

A bridge connects **Valentia Island**, with its high slate cliffs, to the mainland at Portmagee. The island was the European terminus of the first Atlantic cable (1866), making possible the first telegraphic contact with America.

Off Valentia, the Skelligs Rocks rise abruptly from the ocean, shrouded with mystery and birds. Take a trip to the Skelligs Heritage Centre or tour the islands in a boat.

On the north shore of the peninsula, hills plunge to sea level and cliffs complete the descent. **Dingle Bay** seems startlingly wide and the Dingle Peninsula looks like another country.

From Glenbeigh to Killorglin, the head of the bay is almost totally protected from the rough sea by huge sandbars extending from either shore. **Rossbeigh Strand**, with its 6km (4 miles) of golden sand, is a dream beach.

Crag Cave

To the east of Tralee, the town of Castleisland is the location of the Crag Cave (daily mid-Mar–1 Nov). Nearly 4km (2.5 miles) long and bristling with stalagmites and stalactites, this is one of the best show caves in Ireland.

The last town on the ring, **Killorglin**, saves all its energy for three days in August and a boisterous pagan pageant called the Puck Fair, during which time a mountain goat presides over round-the-clock festivities. To the north, **Tralee ㉓**, the administrative centre of County Kerry, owes its fame to the songwriter William Mulchinock (1820–64). *The Rose of Tralee* and its author are honoured in a monument in the town park. The rose also calls the tune of Tralee's annual festival in late August, when girls of Irish descent from many countries compete in a beauty contest, and the winner is crowned Rose of Tralee.

Slea Head on the Dingle Pensinsula

Kerry County Museum (June–Aug daily 9.30am–5.30pm; Sept–May Tue–Sat; charge; www.kerrycountymuseum.ie) in Tralee offers three experiences all in one. Kerry in Colour is an audiovisual presentation of the splendours of Kerry; the County Museum details Kerry's history since 5000BC; and the Geraldine Experience reconstructs life in medieval Tralee.

Tralee is the principal gateway to the **Dingle Peninsula**, a long, dramatic finger which points some 48km (30 miles) into the Atlantic Ocean. On the south shore, amidst rocky coves, a sandbar grows into an arc of beach jutting more than halfway across the bay. **Inch Strand's** 6km (4 miles) of sand slide gently into the sea. Behind the bathers, archaeologists potter about the dunes, where inhabitants of prehistoric ages left meaningful clues about their way of life.

The small fishing port and resort of **Dingle** ❷ (officially known as An Daingean, the name to look for on signposts) claims to be the most westerly town in Europe. From here to land's end all the hamlets are Irish-speaking parts of the Gaeltacht *(see page 123)*, where folklore and traditional language are still preserved. This is very harsh farming country, where old stone walls are overrun with shrubs and rugged hedges divide skimpy parcels of land into fields. You'll see the sheep grazing on even the most precipitous of hills.

The western part of the peninsula is rich territory for archaeologists. In one area, the Fahan group alone consists of an astonishing 400 *clocháns* (beehive-shaped stone huts), along with forts and other ancient structures. For a spectacular panorama, drive up the **Conor Pass** (at an altitude of 460m/1,500ft) and see the sea out to the north and south, and mountains and lakes on the east and west sides. In this part of the world you're isolated from everything but the wild fuschia and heather beside the road.

THE WEST

Limerick and Clare

By the time the waters of the River Shannon have reached **Limerick** ❷ in the west, they have flowed over 274km (170 miles) through thick and thin, from narrow streams and howling rapids to lakes and lochs. After Limerick they still have another 97km (60 miles) to travel through the estuary to the open Atlantic.

Limerick's position at the meeting of the river and its tidal waters assured the city a long and often violent history. The Danes were first on the scene. Their belligerence provoked repeated attacks by the native Irish, who finally drove them out.

The Anglo-Normans in turn captured *Luimneach* – in English 'Bare Spot'. King John visited in 1210 and ordered the construction of a **bridge** and **King John's Castle** (daily Mar–Apr and Oct 9.30am–5pm; May–Sept 9.30am–5pm; charge; www.shannonheritage.com), which still survive and have been extensively renovated. A riverside footpath runs from the Tourist Office on Arthur's Quay to the castle, passing the Hunt Museum and St Mary's Cathedral en route. The city endured its most memorable siege after the Battle of the Boyne (1690), when Irish supporters of James II *(see page 19)* retired to Limerick pursued by William of Orange. The losers lost again, but the Treaty of Limerick allowed them to leave with honour and guaranteed the Irish freedom of religion. This was repudiated by the English Parliament, so today Limerick carries the title of 'City of the Violated Treaty'.

King John's Castle in Limerick

The 800-year-old **St Mary's Cathedral** (daily 9am–5pm, Nov–Feb until 1pm) has an arched Irish-Romanesque west door, while 15th-century carved misericords under the choir seats show free-ranging imagination with representations of angels, animals and other figures in relief. The waterfront Custom House is now the Hunt Museum (Mon–Sat 10am–5pm, Sun 2–5pm; charge; www.hunt museum.com), housing an outstanding collection of Celtic and medieval treasures and a selection of 20th-century Irish and European art.

Shannon Airport reinforces Limerick's historic role as a centre of commerce. It opened in 1945, making its mark before fast, non-stop transatlantic travel became common. Waiting passengers were offered the chance to buy luxury goods exempt from tax. Thus the world's first duty-free shop grew into a shopping centre.

Bunratty Castle ㉖ (daily, 9am–5.30pm; charge; www. shannonheritage.com) is a busy tourist attraction about 5km (3 miles) from the airport. At night professional Irish entertainers in period costumes recreate medieval banquets for visitors.

A favourite attraction at Bunratty is the **Folk Park** (same hours as the castle) containing replicas of typical old houses of the Shannon region. The peat fires are kept burning, as if the people had just stepped out to milk a cow or catch a fish.

Barren Burren

A frustrated general serving Oliver Cromwell famously condemned the desolate Burren as having 'not enough wood to hang a man, not enough water to drown him, not enough clay to cover his corpse'.

Ennis, the county town of county Clare, has a 13th-century friary, which in the Middle Ages had 350 friars and 600 students. The buildings were expanded over the years, and fully renovated in the 1950s.

The Burren

Northwest of Ennis, around 520 sq km (200 sq miles) of
County Clare belongs to **the Burren** ㉗. Glaciers and ages
of erosion have created limestone pavements – horizontal
slabs divided by fissures, like the aftermath of an earth-
quake. Though sometimes described as a moonscape, the
Burren is anything but barren; it is a quiet world of small
animals, birds, butterflies and alpine and Mediterranean
flowers. It may seem hostile to human habitation, but the
profusion of forts and tombs proves it supported a population for several centuries.

Geologists, botanists and archaeologists have field trips on
the pavements, and speleologists enjoy the caves. More than
40km (25 miles) of caves have been fully explored. Most are for
experts only, but anyone can visit **Aillwee Cave**, southeast of
Ballyvaughan (year-round 10am–6pm; by appointment only

The extraordinary landscape of the Burren

in Dec; charge; www.aillweecave.ie). In Kilfenora, a village on the edge of this plain, citizens have established the **Burren Display Centre** as a pleasant way to get your bearings. Kilfenora Cathedral, dating from the 12th century, is noted for its sculptured monuments and high crosses.

The **Cliffs of Moher** ㉘, 10km (6 miles) northwest of Lahinch, tower 215m (700ft) over the Atlantic Ocean. From **O'Brien's Tower** (daily 9.30am–5.30pm; later in summer; charge), an outpost near to the edge, the cliff faces stand above the sea in horizontal layers as easily defined as the storeys of a glass skyscraper. Great waves crash against the foot of the cliff but the thump is heard late, like the report of a distant artillery shell. The cliffs are populated by thousands of seabirds.

The town of **Lisdoonvarna** was once famous as a spa. Today it is chiefly known for its Matchmaking Festival (www.matchmakerireland.com) during September after the harvest, when farmers traditionally took a break from farming to seek a wife. The festival is a light-hearted affair, attracting some 40,000 hopeful visitors annually.

Across the border in County Galway, the area around Gort has a number of literary associations. Lady Gregory, co-founder of the Abbey Theatre, lived in **Coole Park**, now a national forest (all year; free) with a visitor centre (daily end Mar–May and Sept 10am–5pm; June–Aug 10am–6pm; free). The unique 'autograph tree' is inscribed with the initials of some of her famous visitors – Augustus John, John Masefield, Sean O'Casey and one of the few who is instantly recognized by his initials: George Bernard Shaw.

The tribes of Galway

The surnames of the 14 families or 'tribes' of Welsh and Norman descent who controlled medieval Galway are still commonly found in the city: Blake, Bodkin, Browne, D'Arcy, Ffrench, Kirwan, Joyce, Lynch, Morris, Martin, Skerret, Athy, Dean and Ffont.

Galway

The main city of the western province of Connaught, **Galway** ❷❾ is a port, resort, administrative and cultural centre. In medieval times it prospered as a city-state, but withered in the 17th century after prolonged sieges by the forces of Oliver Cromwell and, four decades later, by William of Orange. Remnants of the old glory still shine in a few corners of the renewed city.

The **Collegiate Church of St Nicholas** was begun by the Anglo-Normans in 1320. Following local tradition, Columbus came to pray here before his voyage to America. Today the area around the church is the venue for a lively Saturday morning food and craft market, now an essential feature of Galway life.

A gargoyle on Lynch's Castle in Galway

During Galway's heyday 14 families, mostly of Welsh and Norman descent, formed a sort of medieval Mafia that controlled the economic and political life of the town. Their common enemy, the O'Flaherty family, inspired the inscription (1549) over the old town gate: 'From the fury of the O'Flaherties, good Lord deliver us'.

Of the tribes in Galway, the Lynch family left the most memories and monuments. **Lynch's Castle**, a town house dating from 1600, is decorated with excellent stonework, gargoyles and carved window frames. This rare building has been restored and houses a bank.

Another reminder of the Lynches is the Lynch Memorial Window, with a plaque recounting the macabre story of James Lynch Fitzstephen – Mayor of Galway in 1493 – who condemned and executed his own son, Walter, for murder. Judge Lynch had to be the hangman because nobody else would agree to carry out the sentence.

Galway's Catholic cathedral – whose full name is **Cathedral of Our Lady Assumed into Heaven and St Nicholas** – has a giant dome looming over the city. The classical architecture is misleading; the church was dedicated in 1965. Alongside the cathedral is Galway's **Salmon Weir**, in which salmon fight their way from the sea up to Lough Corrib. From June to July you can see them queueing up for a chance to leap up the falls and follow their instincts to sweet water.

Derryclare Lake in Connemara

In Galway you can also visit the restored one-up, one-down dwelling at Bowling Green where James Joyce's wife, Nora Barnacle, was brought up. It is now home to the **Nora Barnacle House Museum** (mid-May–mid-Sept Tue–Sat 10am–5pm; charge). Photographs, letters, and other memorabilia from the couple's lives make visiting a unique experience.

Galway's seaside suburb, **Salthill**, is a hugely popular resort with rocky seawalls and beaches of fine sand. It's a great place to watch the sun set on Galway Bay; sprawling hills enclose most of the bay, but the Atlantic can be seen to the west.

Twelve Bens

The huge Twelve Bens of Connemara ('ben' is Gaelic for peak) constitute a range of moody mountains mostly inhabited by sheep; the foot-hills are interspersed with bogs and pretty lakes.

Connemara

Lough Corrib, a loch extending 43km (27 miles) north from Galway, is big enough to be whipped by waves when the wind hurtles down the hillside. It's generally shallow and well supplied with islands and fish – salmon, trout, pike and perch. Lough Corrib divides County Galway into two contrasting regions: a fertile limestone plain to the east, and Connemara – a range of dramatic mountains and sparkling lakes – to the west, all enclosed by the coastline of rugged cliffs and pristine beaches.

Much of the south coast of Connemara is an Irish-speaking enclave. This is also the home of the Connemara pony – robust, intelligent and self-reliant. Spanish horses of the 16th century are rumoured to have crossbred with Irish ponies; one version says that the stallions swam ashore from ships of the Spanish Armada wrecked on nearby rocks.

The sky seems to change by the minute in the far west – dazzling sun, fleeting clouds and rain alternating so quickly that photographers have to be constantly at the ready. The capital is the well-placed market town of **Clifden** ③⓪, a base for exploring the nearby lakes and rivers, as well as fine beaches, bogs and mountains. The town's Irish name is *An Clochan*, meaning 'Stepping Stones'. There are so many areas of water around Clifden that you can't tell the genuine sea inlets from the coves of the lakes, except for the seaweed, a plant which features in Irish cooking more than you'd expect. Nearby is **Kylemore Abbey** (daily 10am–5pm; visitor centre free, gardens and abbey charge; www.kylemoreabbey.com), the home of Ireland's Benedictine nuns and one of the most photographed buildings in the country.

Aran Islands

Out in the Atlantic, 48km (30 miles) off Galway, the **Aran Islands** ㉛ are a remote outpost indeed, little more than stone outcrops. In the past islanders had to struggle to survive, cultivating the bleak limestone terrain, which had so little topsoil that they would ship it in from the mainland or scrape it from the cracks between the rocks and mix it with seaweed fertiliser to grow feed for their livestock. Tourism has now improved their fortunes, and though their famous

An aerial view of Inishmore

Aran sweaters are still made here, these days few of them are hand-knitted. All the locals speak Gaelic in their daily life, but can also speak English.

Inishmore, 'the Big Island' as the Aran folk call it, is 14km (9 miles) from tip to tip and only 3km (2 miles) across. From the air – and you can fly there from Galway – you can make out tapestries of tiny fields enclosed by dry-stone walls. Inishmore's one and only real village, **Kilronan**, has a port where ferries from the mainland dock. The fishermen work aboard modern trawlers, but the traditional *currachs*, tar-coated boats with canvas hulls, are still used. This is an island to explore on foot or rented bicycle, available at the pier. If you're in a hurry, you can hire pony traps for guided tours, or the island even has a single motorised taxi which doubles as a school bus.

The remarkable monument of **Dún Aengus** (Mar–Oct daily 10am–6pm; Nov–Feb 10am–4pm; charge), a giant prehistoric fortress on the sheer edge of a cliff some 91m (300ft) high, is about a 15-minute walk across the fields from the road. Three layers of stone walls, the outermost 6m (20ft) high, surround the courtyard 46m (150ft) across. With the ramparts and obstacles set up beyond the wall, the total area covers 4 hectares (11 acres). Even in modern times it would take a rash general to stage an attack on Dún Aengus.

Elsewhere on the islands, among colourful wild flowers, grazing cows, sheep and an abundance of bounding rabbits, there are numerous **archaeological sites** of less importance, that nevertheless have their own diversion to offer. Here you'll find stone forts and groups of primitive stone dwellings, as well as hermits' cells, round towers and ruined churches.

In striking contrast to these traditional structures, a large, glass-walled factory sits in the west of Inishmore. The

Croagh Patrick

time-honoured dexterity of the Aran women has been fully diverted from the local, hardy wool to modern technology; instead they now spend their time manufacturing electronic components.

County Mayo

Rising high above Clew Bay, conical **Croagh Patrick** is Ireland's holy mountain. Every year thousands of pilgrims ascend the imposing summit, most of them on the last Sunday in July. St Patrick is said to have spent Lent here in 441. There are views of the wide bay and the hills of counties Mayo, Clare and Galway.

Westport ❷, at the head of Clew Bay, is an example of 18th-century urban planning. The Mall boulevard follows the Carrowbeg River. Outside the town, the home of the Marquess of Sligo can be visited. **Westport House** (Mar–Oct daily 11.30am–5.30pm; charge; www.westporthouse.ie) is palatial, with paintings, silver and glassware. There is a Pirate Adventure Park with flume rides and dungeons.

Castlebar, a quiet partly Georgian town, is the county town of Mayo. To the east, in Turlough, **The National Museum of Country Life** ❸ (Tue–Sat 10am–5pm, Sun 2–5pm; free; www.museum.ie) houses the National Folklife Collection, a series of hugely entertaining displays illustrating rural life in Ireland from 1850 to about 1950.

Inland, the village of **Knock** (from the Irish *Cnoc Mhuire* – 'Mary's Hill') is a respected place of pilgrimage. In 1879 the townspeople saw an apparition of the Virgin Mary, St Joseph and St John on a south gable of the old parish church. In the centenary year of 1979, pilgrim Pope John Paul II came from Rome to address an open-air mass at Knock with over 400,000 of the faithful. Knock still caters to the pilgrims, with souvenir shops and a museum of folklore and handicrafts. The site of the famous apparition has been enclosed

Cruising The River Shannon

The best place to hire a boat is Carrick-on-Shannon, the capital of County Leitrim and home to the superb Costello Chapel. Downstream, the river runs into Lough Corry, the first of many interconnected lakes in the Shannon basin. **Lough Ree**, halfway down, is 26km (16 miles) long and 11km (7 miles) wide, with deserted wooded islands.

The main cross-country roads ford the Shannon at the central market town of **Athlone**, with a medieval castle overlooking the Shannon Bridge. The town holds a number of festivals and cultural events. At a bend in the river is **Clonmacnoise**, an ancient monastic settlement founded in the 6th century by St Ciaran. Nearby you can follow a 9-km (5.5-mile) trip along the Clonmacnoise & West Offaly Railway.

Just 6km (4 miles) south of Clonmacnoise, a 16-arch bridge marks Shannonbridge; at Shannon Harbour the Grand Canal from Dublin meets the river. Portumna is a fishing and boating resort with a new marina.

Lough Derg is the largest of the Shannon lakes – 40km (25 miles) long and up to 5km (3 miles) wide with islets and fair green hills beyond – a perfect end to the trip. This is just as well because dangerous rapids abound below **Killaloe**, a prudent place to abandon ship. Killaloe was once a great ecclesiastical centre, where **St Flannan's Cathedral** has been restored to its 12th-century glory. The richly carved Romanesque doorway is said to be the entrance to the tomb of King Murtagh O'Brien of Munster (d. 1120). The granite shaft nearby, from about the year 1,000, bears a bilingual inscription in Runic and Ogham letters – a foretaste of today's Irish-English road signs.

in glass, and statues recreate the position of the figures in the vision.

In **Foxford**, the old woollen mill houses an interpretative centre that tells the story of the famine in the area, while near Ballycastle, on the north Mayo cliffs, the pyramid-shaped heritage centre of **Céide Fields** (mid-Mar–Nov daily 10am–5pm, until 6pm June–Sept; charge; www.heritageireland.ie) uncovers the site of one of the area's many prehistoric settlements. The site, dating back to 3000BC, is estimated to be the single largest Stone Age monument in existence in the world today.

The country's biggest island, **Achill** ❸❹, is buffeted by wind and tide, with meagre farms between ominous mountains and rocky shores. Despite this (or because of it) the scenery – from enormous cliffs to superb beaches – is truly magnificent. Achill feels adrift, though you can drive there from the mainland across an unimpressive bridge. Driving on the island's deserted roads can revive the joy of motoring.

Prehistoric graves can be found on the harsh slopes of Achill's overpoweringly high mountain, the 672-m (2,204-ft) **Slievemore**. Driving offers the most vertigo-inducing cliff views and perspectives of the ocean churning round the off-islands and shoals. Inland, note the three-chimneyed cottages set between moors and bogs.

Shamrock Curtain

Travelling in the west of Ireland you may cross the Shamrock Curtain, an important cultural frontier. Signs are printed in Gaelic letters and the people speak Irish as a first language. This is the Gaeltacht. Its residents strive to maintain Irish as a living language. The Dublin government actively supports Gaeltacht efforts to keep the old language and culture alive. Courses in Irish are offered here every summer.

THE NORTHWEST

Sligo ③⑤ lies between two mountains, Ben Bulben and Knocknarea. The Vikings invaded here in 807. In 1252 Maurice Fitzgerald, the Earl of Kildare, founded **Sligo Abbey** (mid-Mar–Oct daily 10am–6pm; Nov–Dec Fri–Sun 9.30am–4.30pm; charge), a Dominican friary. It burned down in 1414, but was soon rebuilt. It was attacked by Puritan troops in 1641, and the friars were killed. Its ruins combine desolation and grace. Three sides remain, and there are fine carvings.

Sligo town

The resort of **Strandhill**, west of Sligo, has a beach with long-rolling waves for surfers. **Knocknarea**, the flat-topped mountain over this stretch of shore, must have had a curious attraction for the early settlers, as the area abounds in megalithic monuments. A steep but manageable climb will bring you to the 328-m (1,078-ft) summit of Knocknarea, where a large cairn is believed to mark the burial place of the 1st-century Queen Maeve of Connaught. This vantage point gives a fantastic, sweeping view across Sligo Bay. Awesome **Ben Bulben** looms in the distance, 526m (1,730ft) high. On its flat top you'll find arctic and alpine plants.

In the shadow of this majestic mountain is the small church of **Drumcliff**, with its turreted belfry. It was the desire of W.B.

Yeats, who spent many childhood summer holidays around Sligo, to be laid to rest in the churchyard, 'Under bare Ben Bulben's head'.

About 27km (17 miles) to the north of Sligo, situated on the approach to the village of Mullaghmore, look out for the stunning **Classiebawn Castle**, which claims the skyline all to itself. This was the summer dwelling of Earl Mountbatten of Burma, who was assassinated by the IRA in 1979 when his fishing boat was blown up just off the shore nearby.

County Donegal

The most northerly county on the island, **Donegal** is known for its scenery – mountains, glens and lakes. This is also where Donegal homespun **tweed** comes from. **Donegal town** ㊱ has a medieval **castle** that occupies the site of a previous Viking fort. (*Dun na nGall* in Irish means the 'Fortress of the

Donegal town has a charming setting

Forcigners', a reference to the Vikings.) On the edge of town, the ruins of Donegal Abbey overlook the estuary. West along the coast, **Killybegs** is a big fishing port; the trawlers here have wheelhouses with devices for tracking down the fish.

Donegal's medieval castle

The road to the village of **Glencolumbkille** ⓷⓻ heads deep into spectacular country. Over the crest of a hill, you see the simple village below, enfolded in green hillsides that funnel down to the sea. In Irish the name *Glencolumbkille* means the 'Glen of St Colmcille' (or St Columba).

Today it is said that the 6th-century saint, who changed the course of history by introducing the Christian faith to Scotland, began his career by converting locals. The numerous old **standing stones** were formerly pagan monuments which St Columba simply adapted to the new religion. On the saint's feast day, 9 June, pilgrims follow the pathway of these old stones. Over 40 prehistoric *dolmens*, *souterrains* and cairns have been catalogued in this area, some as old as 5,000 years.

Between Derry and Letterkenny, you can visit the **stone fort** built in prehistoric times, which is well-preserved and similar in style to Staigue Fort in County Kerry. **Fort Dunree**, on the Inishowen peninsula overlooking Lough Swilly, is a fascinating military history museum in an old fort.

Glenveagh National Park ⓷⓼ forms 10,000 hectares (24,700 acres) of the most beautiful part of Co. Donegal, including Glenveagh Castle and Glebe House, built in 1828 in graceful Regency style and sumptuously furnished. It was once the home of Derek Hill, the artist, who gave it to the Irish nation.

The *Hands Across the Divide* statue in Derry

NORTHERN IRELAND

Surprisingly for such an historically troubled area, it's sometimes hard to be sure of the exact location of the border
between the Republic and Northern Ireland. Partly this is
because it snakes its way along 18th-century county boundaries through farming land that is sometimes bleak, more
often breathtakingly beautiful, taking little account of natural
boundaries such as rivers, or of the cultural differences that
separate Republican-minded Roman Catholics and British-
oriented Protestants. Houses straddle it so that, as the joke has
it, a man may sleep with his head in the United Kingdom and
his heart in the Republic of Ireland.

Political expediency accounts for the absurdities. It had been
intended to redraw the border rationally after partition in 1920
left six of the nine counties of the ancient province of Ulster
(Antrim, Down, Armagh, Derry, Fermanagh and Tyrone) under

British rule, and a Boundary Commission was set up to advise. But in the end the British and Irish governments, both hoping to avoid further trouble, suppressed the commission's report and left things as they were. Had they decided differently, much of the subsequent conflict might have been averted.

Belfast

Belfast , the capital, looks little different from a provincial English city. Donegall Place, its 'main street', is lined with UK chain stores such as Marks & Spencer, Next and Boots; while postboxes and telephone kiosks are no longer green, as in the Republic, but are painted red as they are in Birmingham or Liverpool. Sectarian tensions are a thing of the past: nowadays bus and taxi tours show visitors where the worst riots of the 1970s and '80s took place, a venture that typifies the sharp wit and relentless energy of Belfast's inhabitants.

Set in a saucer of green hills and spanning the mouth of the River Lagan as it flows into the Irish Sea, Belfast is essentially a Victorian creation, its wealth founded on textile manufacturing and shipbuilding. Today most of the factories have vanished, though two towering yellow cranes (Samson and Goliath) survive as a reminder of the great days of Harland & Wolff shipyard, builder of the *Titanic*. The 100th anniversary of the sailing of the pride of Belfast's shipyards, the Titanic took place in April 2012, and was marked by the opening of a new visitor centre.

Shopping in Belfast's bustling centre

Dominating the centre in Donegall Square is the 1906 **City Hall** whose architecture has been dubbed 'Wrenaissance' in tribute to its shameless resemblance to St Paul's Cathedral in London. Queen Victoria presides outside, her statue supported by toilers from the linen and shipbuilding industries. Inside, an ornate marble staircase sweeps up to the Rotunda, and the banqueting hall and council chamber are suitably grandiloquent. Among the marble statues around the City Hall is a **Titanic Memorial**, complete with weeping sea-nymphs.

To the north of the City Hall, Donegall Place, which becomes Royal Avenue, is Belfast's main shopping thoroughfare. **Linen Hall Library B**, on Donegall Square North, is a revered public-subscription library – a treasure house for historians and political journalists. Close by, on Great Victoria Street, are two architectural gems: the 1895 **Grand Opera House C** (www.goh.co.uk), with its plush brass and velvet, its gilded elephant heads and its excellent acoustics, and the

Taking it easy in Linen Hall Library

Crown Liquor Saloon ⓓ, a riot of Victorian Baroque owned by the National Trust but still serving the finest Guinness and whiskies.

Queen's University

Great Victoria Street leads on, via Shaftesbury Square, to the Tudor-style **Queen's University ⓔ**, whose central tower bears a suspicious resemblance to that of Magdalen College, Oxford. The university has colonised just about every available building in the vicinity, but welcome green space is provided by the adjacent **Royal Botanic Gardens ⓕ**, which contain a curvilinear Palm House. Beside the park is the revamped **Ulster Museum ⓖ**, which is noted for its well-presented displays of Irish art from the Bronze Age onwards.

Belfast, of course, has many churches. Worth checking out are the neo-Romanesque **St Anne's Cathedral ⓗ** in Donegall Street, the extravagantly decorated interior of **St Malachy's Church ⓘ** in Clarence Street and the delightful **First Presbyterian Church ⓙ** in Rosemary Street.

Across the River Lagan, in the newly-named Titanic Quarter, the **Odyssey Arena ⓚ** (www.odysseyarena.com) is a venue for sporting events and pop concerts, and hosts the interactive discovery centre, W5 (Mon–Thur 10am–5pm, Fri–Sat 10am–6pm, Sun noon–6pm; charge; www.w5online.co.uk). The city's newest attraction, the **Titanic Belfast ⓛ** (Apr–Sept Mon–Sat 9am–7pm, Sun 10am–5pm; Oct–Mar daily 10am–5pm; charge; www.titanicbelfast.com) relives the liner's story in nine galleries with full-scale reconstructions.

On the Newtownards Road, 10km (6 miles) from the centre, are the much televised **Parliament Buildings** at Stormont,

The Giant's Causeway

echoing the pomp of Buckingham Palace. They are now the home of the Northern Ireland Assembly.

The Antrim Coast Road

To the northeast of Belfast, past **Carrickfergus** (which has a fine Norman castle) and the industrial port of **Larne** ⓐ, the lovely **Antrim Coast Road** runs alongside the Irish Sea through picturesque villages such as **Cushendall** and **Cushendun**. Diversions can be made along the way into any of the nine green glens, peaceful landscapes traditionally farmed.

The north coast begins at **Ballycastle** ⓐ, setting for an end-of-August agricultural fair, held since 1606, and the ferry departure point for a 13-km (8-mile) trip to **Rathlin Island**, whose population of 100 is vastly outnumbered by seabirds. Continuing east, you pass **Carrick-a-Rede Rope Bridge** (daily weather permitting Mar–May and Sept–Oct 10am–6pm; June–Aug 10am–7pm; charge) which swings over a 24-m (80-ft) chasm, allowing salmon fishermen and brave tourists access to a rocky promontory. Past cliffs and white surfers' beaches are the romantic ruins of the 6th-century **Dunseverick Castle**.

Bushmills is home to the world's oldest distillery (tours and whiskey tastings available). It is also the jumping-off point for Ireland's most spectacular natural phenomenon, the **Giant's Causeway** ❷. Formed 60 million years ago when molten lava froze into 38,000 basalt columns, mostly hexagonal, it looks like a series of giant stepping-stones. Park near the Causeway or, in season, catch a narrow-gauge steam locomotive from Bushmills. To the west are the resorts of **Portrush** and **Portstewart**, and the ruins of the 14th-century **Dunluce Castle**, perched on a crumbling cliff.

Derry City and Fermanagh

Protestants still call **Derry** ❸, Northern Ireland's second city, Londonderry, the name given to it by the London guilds who began creating the walled city in 1614. The 6-m (20-ft) thick

Music and Murals

Northern Ireland's popular culture portrays the sectarian divide with the bluntness of bombs and bullets. Triumphalist or threatening murals adorn the sides of hundreds of houses, particularly in Belfast and Derry. The Protestant versions often feature William of Orange, who defeated his Catholic father-in-law, James II, at the Battle of the Boyne in 1690. Catholic murals celebrate Republican heroes and aspirations. Balaclava-clad men brandishing rifles are common to both traditions. The worst murals are crudely executed; the best can be evaluated as folk art.

For both Protestants and Catholics, marching bands keep history alive and mark out territory. The biggest parades are staged on 12 July by Protestant Orangemen (commemorating William of Orange). On the surface it's tuneful pageantry – but it can also be fiercely provocative.

Derry/Londonderry

walls boast watchtowers and cannons, such as the 1642 'Roaring Meg'. The excellent **Tower Museum**, in Union Hall Place, relates the city's troubled history. **St Columb's Cathedral**, in London Street, is a graceful 17th-century Anglican church.

3.5km (5 miles) north of Omagh is the **Ulster-American Folk Park** ⓮ (Tue–Fri 10am–4pm, Sat and Sun 11am–4pm; charge; www.nmni.com). The rebuilt crafts-men's cottages, schoolhouse and forge recreate 18th-century living conditions here, while log cabins and covered wagons illus-trate the New World that many emigrants created in America. It is said that 11 US presidents had their roots in the province.

Further south, **Fermanagh** is the province's lakeland play-ground. Summer pleasure boats ply the lakes from the busy county town of **Enniskillen** ⓯. On Lower Lough Erne, **Boa Island** has an ancient two-faced Janus statue, radiating Celtic inscrutability, and **Devenish Island** has a fine round tower.

Heading back towards the east coast, it's worth stopping at **Armagh** ⓰, which has two fine cathedrals (both called St Patrick's), some notable Georgian buildings and a planetarium. Just outside the town is **Navan Fort**, Europe's oldest Celtic site.

Mountains of Mourne

Close to the Irish Sea, the 15 granite peaks of the **Mourne Mountains** ⓱ reach to more than 600m (2,000ft). At the summit of Slieve Donard are two cairns (ancient mounds of stones). From here, on a clear day, you can see Scotland, England, the Isle of Man and Snowdonia in Wales.

Passing through **Downpatrick**, a sedate market town, you can take the ferry from Strangford to Portaferry and drive up the **Ards Peninsula** ㊽ a 37-km (23-mile) finger dotted by villages and beaches. **Mount Stewart**, an 18th-century mansion, has one of Europe's greatest gardens (Mar–Oct), its microclimate nourishing a vast variety of plants, shrubs and trees.

At Cultra, near Holywood on the main road into Belfast, the **Ulster Folk and Transport Museum** ㊾ (Tue–Fri, 10am–4pm, Sat and Sun 11am–4pm; charge; www.nmni.com) is set in 70 hectares (170 acres) of a green and picnic-friendly woodland park. Old farmhouses, mills and even a church were moved with painstaking labour, stone by stone, from their original sites all over Ulster to be preserved in one spot, forming an agricultural, industrial and social history. The large and impressive transport collection contains old carriages and bicycles, steam locomotives, cars and aircraft.

A recreated shop in the Ulster Folk and Transport Museum

WHAT TO DO

SPORTS

Whether on land or sea (or river or lake), the Irish enjoy so many sporting activities that we can only touch on a handful of the most popular. If you are interested in more esoteric sports, such as kite-surfing, hang-gliding, or even polo, the tourist board *(see page 129)* can put you in touch with the appropriate sports associations.

Sports Ashore

Golf. In a country so green, you might scarcely notice the vast number of golf courses, but there are more than 600, including several of championship status. Some clubs are private, but not rigorously so: while you might find that non-members are excluded over the weekend, you'll have few problems on weekdays. See www.golfingireland.com for more details.

Greyhound racing. This is a very popular pursuit. Teams of hare-brained dogs keep eager gamblers busy six nights a week in Dublin – which has two greyhound stadiums – and elsewhere in Ireland. See http://greyhoundracing.ie.

Horse racing. Almost everyone in Ireland seems to be totally engrossed, one way or another, in the sport of kings. Dublin boasts several famous courses within easy reach. The flat season is from March to November, and steeplechasing goes on all year. See www.goracing.ie for information on events.

Horse riding. Stables can be found all over Ireland with fine Irish horses, beautiful ponies, and trekking routes through delightful verdant countryside; www.ehi.ie lists establishments that specially cater for holiday makers.

Walking in the Mourne Mountains

Hurling is a popular Gaelic game

National games. Hurling is a very fast variant of hockey, in which a small, leather-covered ball is struck with a wooden hurley. Gaelic football, the other traditional Irish game, includes elements of both soccer and rugby. For more information on Gaelic sporting events and history, go to www.gaa.ie.

Imported games. Rugby (www.irishrugby.ie) and football (www.fai.ie) leagues are very popular, and cricket is also played.

Walking and cycling. Both have grown in popularity, with some 32 long-distance walking routes, and numerous dedicated cycle routes. See www.discoverirelandie/walking or /cycling.

Sports on the Water

Sailing. Watersports of all kinds are popular in Ireland, with its long indented coastline. Hire a yacht with or without skipper, or get afloat in a simple kayak. See www.discover ireland.ie.

Scuba diving. It's popular all around Ireland – mostly in the summer months, as the water can get mighty cold. Along the north coast, there are lots of wreck dives: many believe that Spanish galleons from the Armada are still lurking beneath the waves. For a list of dive centres see www. scuba.ie.

Sea fishing. From a long sandy beach, a pier, a clifftop or a boat, you can hook big beautiful trophies of the deep, such as shark, sea bass, tope, skate, halibut, conger and many more. Details at www.discoverireland.com/angling.

Swimming. Blue Flag beaches have to meet certain safety criteria, including having adequate life-saving equipment and, if necessary, lifeguards. For a list of Blue Flag beaches all over Ireland, visit www.blueflag.org.

Surfing. The heavy Atlantic swells are more impressive on the west coast, where the biggest surfing bases are Lahinch Co. Clare, Strandhill Co. Sligo, Bundoran Co. Donegal, and Tramore Co. Waterford. See www.surfaroundireland.com.

Boating. Cruising the inland waterways in a rented cabin cruiser makes a great break, especially on the River Shannon. You can also try more energetic sports such as canoeing on lakes or rivers. See www.discoverireland.ie.

Game fishing. Fertile salmon fisheries are mostly restricted, but arrangements can be made – though preferably well in advance. Trout are abundant in rivers and lakes; as with salmon, you will need a licence. Details at www.discoverirelandcom/angling.

Riding ponies on Cleggan Beach in Connemara

SHOPPING

Friendly sales staff help make shopping in Ireland a real pleasure. The appealing products here are made by Irish craftsmen in traditional or new styles; the Kilkenny Design Centre in Kilkenny City has a particularly fine range of traditional goods on offer. The Crafts Council's website at www.ccoi.ie is also a good starting point that enables you to research what's available in the area you're visiting.

Celtic details on souvenirs

For clothes or slightly more eclectic souvenirs, Dublin is the place to visit. It offers shoppers everything from upscale boutiques to huge shopping malls: check out the vast new **Dundrum Town Centre**, just outside Dublin city centre, or the more intimate **Powerscourt Centre**. Grafton Street is the main shopping street, with high street names and fashionable department stores such as the much-loved Brown Thomas. Other interesting shops include the **House of Names**, Nassau Street, whose handmade coats of arms allegedly feature the crests of more than 96 percent of the world's surnames; **Celtic Note**, also on Nassau Street, a delight for music lovers with everything from traditional to contemporary, via Riverdance; and **George's Street Arcade**, just off South Great George's, a vibrant indoor market with an eclectic worldwide mix from Greek olives to Peruvian handwoven rugs.

What to Buy

Aran sweaters. These fishermen's sweaters can be easily recognised. Demand so far exceeds supply that they are now made in mainland factories as well as in the cottages on the Aran islands. Be sure to check your garment is genuinely handknitted.

Connemara marble. A rich green, this stone is made into all sorts of souvenirs.

Chocolate. Buy delicious hand-made chocolates at Butler's Irish Chocolates in Grafton Street, Dublin, and at the Skelligs Chocolate Co. in Ballinskelligs, County Kerry. Try before you buy at the Lir Cafés in Killarney, County Kerry and Carrigaline, County Cork. The Chocolate Room in Belfast is the place to head for sweet souvenirs in Northern Ireland.

Crafts. Enamel dishes, plaques and pendants by local crafters.

Crosses. Reproductions of old Christian crosses and St Brigid crosses made out of straw.

Dolls. Dressed in traditional regional costumes.

Glassware. Waterford crystal, world renowned, is still available even though the factory has closed. Jerpoint Glass in County Kilkenny produces hand-blown uncut crystal in contemporary designs.

Beautiful local glassware

Jewellery. Celtic designs and illustrations from the ancient Book of Kells inspire today's goldsmiths and silversmiths, while others work in a contemporary style.

Traditionally woven baskets
for sale in Dublin

Lace. Although a waning trade in Limerick and County Monaghan, there is now a strong revival of lace-making in Carrickmacross, Clones, Kenmare and Youghal.

Linen. Weaving continues in Northern Ireland and is sold everywhere in the country. The Brown Thomas department store in Dublin, Cork and Galway stock a great range of linen clothes.

Paintings. Artists produce fine studies of Ireland, including landscapes, seascapes, flora and fauna, in oils, watercolours and pen and wash. Works are widely available and well priced.

Peat. Even the turf of Ireland is compressed and sculpted to reproduce ancient religious and folklore symbols.

Pottery. Traditional and modern designs in kitchenware, sought after by collectors.

Rushwork. In a land rich in thatched cottages, the makers of woven baskets and similar wickerwork still thrive.

Smoked salmon. A souvenir you can eat that is specially packed for travelling, and on sale at the airport.

Souvenirs. Leprechauns in all sizes, worry stones made of marble, elegant Irish coffee glasses and *shillelaghs* (short wooden clubs) are all widely available. Books about every aspect of Irish life and its history make easy-to-carry souvenirs.

Tweed. Handwoven fabrics in a variety of colours and weights, ideal for overcoats, jackets or light shawls.

Wood turning. Many wood turners use only storm-damaged timber, making an ecologically sound product.

ENTERTAINMENT

Traditional Music

Many hotels and pubs provide entertainment, featuring the most diverse cross-section of traditional Irish entertainment possible: folk singers, harpists, dancers and storytellers. In local pubs the programme may consist of a lone folk singer with guitar. At the other end of the scale the luxury hotels put on elaborate productions. The shows have a typically Irish mixture of hand-clapping high spirits and 'Come Back to Erin' nostalgia. Jigs and reels are tirelessly danced, and lively tap dancers revive some of the country's oldest and best routines. Harps and banjos, bagpipes and accordions are all played with gusto, and fast fiddlers are as ubiquitous here as gypsy violinists in Budapest.

You will find less polished versions of traditional Irish music at *fleadhanna*, festivals of music and song around the

A traditional Irish music performance in the Tigh Naechtain pub, Galway

island, climaxing in the All Ireland *Fleadh* in the summer (August). Tourist offices will have detailed schedules of such events (wwwfleadhnua.com).

Clubs and Bars

The traditional pub is the heartbeat of Irish life and you can still find the real thing all over the country. Escape the gastropubs to traditional drinking holes like Dublin's ancient Brazen Head on Bridge Street and, in Belfast, the Crown Liquor Saloon on Great Victoria Street *(see page 83)*. Both will be full of tourists, but a great experience all the same.

Dublin has a lively clubbing scene, centring on the Temple Bar area. The better clubs have world-class DJs nightly, plus regular live acts. The Button Factory (ww2.buttonfactory.ie) features a wide range of live music, and late-night themed events attracting a young crowd. Older sophisticates will enjoy the atmosphere at The Sugar Club on Leeson Street (www.the sugarclub.com).

Medieval Mayhem

Restored medieval castles are used for grandiose candlelit **banquets** with traditional stories, poems and songs. These recreations of lusty celebrations from the past are professionally arranged. If you have no car you can join package tours that include door-to-door transportation. Popular venues include Bunratty and Knappogue Castles in County Clare and Dunguaire Castle in County Galway: www.shannonheritage.com.

Theatre

Ireland's grand **theatrical** tradition – which gave the world Goldsmith, Shaw, Sheridan, Beckett, O'Casey and more recently Conor McPherson and Martin McDonagh – continues in major towns such as Dublin, Belfast and Cork. Tickets are usually available on the night at Ireland's National

Theatre. The Abbey Theatre Dublin (www.abbeytheatre.ie) is still packing them in after more than 100 years. See www.entertainment.ie for full listings of concerts, theatre and film.

CHILDREN

Fun activities for children of all ages can be found throughout the country at:
- **Bray promenade**, 19km (12 miles) south of Dublin. A big seaside resort with dodgems and a seafront aquarium.
- **Bunratty Castle and Folk Park**, County Clare, tel: (061) 360 788, www.shannonheritage.com. Costumed guides recreate life in olden times. Open daily year-round.
- **Clara-Lara**, Vale of Clara, County Wicklow, tel: (0404) 46161, www.claralara.com. Fun park, trout farm and amusements for children of all ages. Open summer only.

Co Clare's beaches are great fun for children

There is plenty to entertain children in Dublin

- **Dublin Zoo**, tel: (01) 474 8900, www.dublinzoo.ie. A wide variety of animals. Café and restaurant.
- **Farm visits**. Many farms open to visitors and are ideal for kids. Tourist information offices *(see page 129)* have details.
- **Exploris**, Portaferry, County Down, tel: (028) 4272 8062, www.exploris.org.uk. Discover creatures of the deep.
- **Fota Wildlife Park**, near Cobh, County Cork, tel: (021) 481 2678, www.fotawildlife.ie. This large park opens year-round.
- **National Gallery of Ireland**, Dublin, tel: (01) 661 5133, www.nationalgallery.ie. Frequent children's activities.
- **National Wax Museum**, Dublin, tel: (01) 872 6340 www.waxmuseumplu.ie. Historical and celebrity wax figures.
- **Newbridge Demesne**, County Dublin, tel: (01) 843 6534. An 18th-century house with farm and animals.
- **Straffan Butterfly Farm**, County Kildare, tel: (01) 627 1109, www.straffanbutterflyfarm.com. Lots of butterflies as well as tarantulas, snakes and scorpions. Open June–Aug.
- **The Steam Museum**, Straffan, County Kildare, tel: (01) 628 8412, www.steam-museum.ie, has model and full-sized steam engines; open June–Aug (May and Sept by appointment).
- **Kerry County Museum**, tel: (066) 712 7777, www.kerry museum.ie, in Tralee has a child-friendly Medieval Experience complete with sounds and smells of a medieval town.
- **Viking Splash Tours**, Dublin, tel: (01) 707 6000, www.viking splash.ie. Put on a Viking helmet and explore land and sea in a vintage World War II amphibious vehicle.

Calendar of Events

Contact local tourist offices for latest information on particular festivals.

January: Temple Bar Trad-Irish Music and Culture Festival, Dublin – includes family events and evening gigs; Shindig Festival, Tralee – Irish dancing lessons, storytelling and singing.

February: Jameson Dublin International Film Festival; Circus Festival Ireland, Cork City – watch and learn circus skills.

March: St Patrick's Week – celebrations throughout Ireland.

March–April: Pan-Celtic International Festival, Donegal, Co. Donegal – a celebration of Celtic tradition through music, song, dance, language and sport; the famous Irish Grand National horse race.

April: The Cork International Choral Festival. Waterford Celebrates Food – a weekend of tastings and demonstrations.

May: Irish Open Golf Championships; Fleadh Nua Music Festival, Ennis, Co. Clare; Dundalk International Maytime Festival – theatre and music performances; Listowel Writers Week, Co. Kerry; Slieve Bloom Walking Festival – breathtaking guided mountain walks for every level.

June: Music in Great Irish Houses Chamber Music Festival, all over Ireland; Cork Midsummer Festival – huge arts festival with promenade theatre'. Irish Derby at the Curragh race course, Co. Kildare.

July: Galway Races and Arts Festival; Lady of the Lake Festival, Enniskillen; Kinsale Arts Week.

August: Connemara Pony Show, Clifden, Co. Galway; Kilkenny Arts Festival; Oul' Lammas Fair, Ballycastle, Co. Antrim; Puck Fair – three days and nights of Irish entertainment, Killorglin, Co. Kerry; Stradbally Steam Rally, Co. Laois; Rose of Tralee International Festival, Kerry

September: Guinness All Ireland Senior Hurling Final, Dublin; Festival of Light Opera, Waterford; Clarenbridge Oyster Festival, Galway; Lisdoonvarna Matchmaking Festival, Co. Clare – traditional matchmakers pair up singletons amid music and dancing.

October: International Gourmet Festival, Kinsale, Co. Cork; Dublin Theatre; Ballinasloe Fair, Co. Galway – Europe's oldest horse fair; Cork Jazz Festival; Belfast Festival at Queen's, huge arts festival.

EATING OUT

Pubs are popular lunch or dinner spots and they range from traditional taverns serving up sandwiches and salads to cosmopolitan gastro pubs. Cafés provide relaxed brunches and afternoon teas and there are luxurious restaurants offering Michelin-starred cuisine. Vegetarians are pretty well catered for these days, and the trend for locally-sourced artisan food has greatly enhanced the choice at all price levels.

Dublin's days of overcooked cabbage and cholesterol-laden fried meat are long gone. The city is increasingly sophisticated in its array and quantity of restaurants, and is matching other European capitals as a breeding ground for talented and innovative chefs. It can be expensive, though.

Cork's English Market

Kinsale, a small town in County Cork, and Kenmare, a village in County Kerry have both been called the 'gourmet capital' of Ireland. Cork and Galway have a good choice of casual city centre restaurants, while Belfast takes its culinary reputation seriously, and has a wide choice of adventurous eateries. Outside Dublin and Belfast ethnic restaurants in Ireland tend to be expensive and run-of-the-mill.

Alfresco dining

You don't have to look far to find an idyllic setting for a picnic in Ireland. Farmhouse cheeses, smoked salmon, freshly baked bread and fresh produce supply the ingredients and the scenery is provided by a long and winding coast, over 400 forest areas and moody mountain views that will seldom let you down even if the weather does.

Ireland's Blue Book of Country Houses is a good source for exploring Ireland's famous castle hotels and stately homes. Don't miss the chance to enjoy a meal at one of Dublin's top restaurants. Lunch is often half the price of dinner and may include specials.

If you're on a budget, there are many small cafés and tearooms which provide good value. Look out for pubs offering 'carvery lunches' – a self-service option with generous portions of the roast of the day, a choice of potatoes, and assorted vegetables for under €10.

There is also the ever-present chippy. Often the traditional end to a night in the pub, they also make a cheap, tasty and quick option to eating out. Thanks to the long coastline, the fish is always fresh and often cooked to order.

In addition to VAT (value added tax, 13.5 percent or 17.5 percent in Northern Ireland), some upmarket restaurants add a service charge to the bill; extra tips are given at about 10 percent of the total bill.

When to Eat

Breakfast is served from about 7–10am, though in some hotels, matching the general leisurely air, it does not begin until 8am.

Lunchtime is from 12.30–2.30pm, give or take half an hour at either end. The time of the evening meal depends on where you are. In rural areas and perhaps the less sophisticated town areas, people dine as early as 6pm. In the major towns and cities, however, you can eat any time from 6 or 7–10pm.

What to Eat
Breakfast

A real Irish breakfast starts the day superlatively. You'll feel ready for any kind of exertion after a menu of juice, porridge, or cold cereal with milk or cream, fried eggs with bacon and sausages, toast or tasty homemade soda bread, butter, marmalade, tea or coffee. The quality of the bacon and sausages has improved enormously with the surge in artisan butchers.

In Ulster an important constituent of the breakfast fry-up is fried *farl* (potato bread). Irish soda bread, white or brown, is made from flour and buttermilk, bicarbonate of soda and salt; it's as delicious as cake. Black pudding, a heavy sausage filled with grains and blood, is a treat you'll either love or hate.

Irish stew

Other Meals

Irish **soups** are usually thick and hearty: vegetables, barley and meat stock with a dab of cream, for instance. Look for potato soup made of potatoes, onions, carrots and parsley.

Fish caught fresh from the Atlantic, the Irish Sea or the island's streams is incredibly good. Keep an eye out for some of these

Galway Bay oysters

great Irish delights: fresh salmon (poached or grilled), smoked salmon, sole and trout from the sea and rivers. Dublin Bay prawns are a big natural resource worthy of their fame, as are Galway oysters (often accompanied by a bottle of stout). With luck you could be offered mussels or lobster, but the great bulk of the catch is usually exported to the Continent.

Meat of the highest quality is at the centre of Irish cuisine. As is common in restaurants around the world, it is generally served simply to allow the fine flavour to speak for itself. The beef is excellent, but there is very little veal. You'll have a choice of roast beef or sumptuous steaks (either T-bone, filet mignon or sirloin) served with elegant sauces, seasonal vegetables and fondant potatoes. Lamb appears as tender chops or as a roast, or the main ingredient in Irish stew, a filling casserole of meat, potatoes, carrots and onions, laced with parsley and thyme. Irish pork products – bacon, sausages, chops and

Limerick ham – are also rightly famous. Dublin coddle is a delicious stew of sausages, bacon, onions, potatoes and parsley, a favourite for Saturday night supper in the capital. Venison is another popular choice at quality restaurants, as is rabbit or hare.

Potatoes have been a mainstay of the Irish diet since the 17th century, and a choice of roast, mashed and garlic potatoes or chips with your main course is not unusual. Mushrooms, which thrive in the cool, humid atmosphere here, are the single biggest horticultural export.

More and more restaurants are now serving vegetarian dishes, and fresh produce from Ireland's farms is a dream come true for those thinking Irish food is nothing more than meat and dairy.

Desserts are often similar to English puddings – sweet, sticky and served with lashings of thick cream or ice cream.

Fresh produce for sale

What to Drink

A jug of tap water is often found on the table, and for many diners it's the only drink during the meal. Ireland has many brands of bottled spring water, widely sold in pubs and restaurants, and water is gaining popularity as a substitute for alcoholic drinks, especially at lunchtime. Some restaurants have a full licence to serve any drinks; otherwise, they serve wine only and not beer.

The Palace Bar in Fleet Street, Dublin

Irish **pubs** are usually as relaxed and friendly as their regular clients. Most are open all day, and most also serve tea and freshly made coffee. In rural areas the pub may not open until 6pm or later. Closing time is normally around midnight; sometimes later on Friday and Saturday nights. Pubs serving food or providing entertainment can apply for a licence to open later still. Some pubs in Northern Ireland may be shut on Sundays.

The Irish drink nearly 500 million pints of **beer** a year, mostly stout – a rich, creamy, dark brown version. Cork's two brands of stout, Beamish and Murphy's, have become increasingly popular. In many a pub the simple order 'a pint, please' means 568 ml of **Guinness**, lovingly drawn from the keg, scraped and topped. The pouring and settling process takes a little time, but it's worth the wait. The head is so thick that the barman can leave the image of a shamrock sitting within it. A 'glass' of stout means half a pint.

Irish lagers and ales are less filling, and are also worth trying. An interesting Irish drink, **Black Velvet**, combines stout and champagne, and is said to be good for hangovers.

The word **whiskey** comes from the Gaelic *uisce beatha*, 'water of life'. (Purists are at pains to spell Irish whiskey with an 'e' unlike the Scottish version.) Whiskey is matured in wooden casks for at least seven years and is drunk neat, or with a little water – never with ice. You'll see the names of Irish whiskeys etched in the glass of pub windows.

Enthusiasts can visit the world's oldest whiskey distillery, Bushmills (www.bushmills.com), in Northern Ireland; it has held a licence since 1609. There's also the Old Jameson Distillery in Smithfield, the heart of old Dublin, and the Old Midleton Distillery just outside Cork; both are owned by Jameson. For further information go to www.jameson whiskey. com.

The Old Jameson Distillery in Smithfield, Dublin

Whiskey features in many of Ireland's unusual and delicious drinks: **Irish coffee**, in a stemmed glass, is hot coffee laced with whiskey and sugar, with a tablespoonful of thick cream floating on top.

Two Irish liqueurs merit a try: **Irish mist** – honey and herbs in a whiskey base – tingles on the palate, and **Irish cream liqueur**, in different brands, is also very popular with coffee: there's Bailey's and Carolan's, Sheridan's and St Brendan's. It contains whiskey, chocolate and cream – like a leprechaun's milkshake, they say.

PLACES TO EAT

To give you an idea of prices, we have used the following symbols for a three-course meal for one excluding wine:

€€€ over €40   £££ over £35
€€ €20–40   ££ £15–35
€ under €20   £ under £15

DUBLIN

Chapter One Restaurant €€–€€€ *18/19 Parnell Square, Dublin 1, tel: (01) 873 2266, www.chapteronerestaurant.com, open for lunch (12.30–2.30pm, Tue–Fri) and dinner (6–11pm, Tue–Sat).* This establishment, in the basement of the Dublin Writers Museum, is one of the city's best. The menu is classically French, but with a leaning toward Irish. It takes its cheeses and wines very seriously, and it shows. Located just across from the Gate Theatre, there are pre-theatre menus available from 6pm. Reservations advised.

Cornucopia € *19 Wicklow Street, Dublin 2, tel: (01) 677 7583, www.cornucopia.ie, open Mon–Sat 8.30am–8pm (Thur until 9pm), Sun noon–7pm.* A small vegetarian restaurant offering simple, delicious meals such as Turkish bean casserole, tasty salads and wholemeal breads. Great place for breakfast too.

Elephant and Castle €–€€ *18 Temple Bar, Dublin 2, tel: (01) 679 3121, www.elephantandcastle.ie, open Mon–Fri 8am–11.30pm, Sat–Sun 10.30am–11.30pm.* This is the most popular informal restaurant in the city. Quality burgers, salads and meals with a hint of Mexican or Thai influence are on offer. Vegetarian options.

Ely Winebar, €€ *22 Ely Place, St Stephen's Green, Dublin 2, tel (01) 676 8986, www.elywinebar.ie, open lunch and dinner Mon–Fri noon–11.30pm, Sat 5pm–12.30am.* Experience the elegance of old Dublin in this classic wine-bar restaurant near the Shelbourne Hotel. Over 70 wines served by the glass, and organic food from the family farm.

Fallon & Byrne €–€€ *11-17 Exchequer Street, Dublin 2, tel (01) 472 1010, www.fallonandbyrne.com, Restaurant open Mon–Sat 12.30–3pm, 6–10pm, Sun noon–4pm.* Organic food emporium in former telephone exchange. Choose from the ground floor take-away deli, tapas in the cellar bar or the French brasserie on the spacious top floor.

Old Dublin Restaurant €€–€€€ *90–1 Francis Street, Dublin 8, tel: (01) 454 2028, open lunch Mon–Fri 12.30–2.15pm, dinner Mon–Sat 6–11pm.* Specialising in Russian and Scandinavian recipes such as *novgorod* (beef chateaubriand with fried barley and caviar) and *pelmini* (small beef or veal dumplings in consommé), this is an unusual but long-established restaurant. Book in advance.

CORK

Ballymaloe House €€€ *Shanagarry, tel: (021) 465 2531, www. ballymaloe.ie, open daily with lunch served at 1pm, dinner between 7.30–9.30pm (8.30pm Sun).* Located on a farm and run by the Allen family, noted for their gourmet cooking. Meals are served in the house's cosy dining rooms and waiting guests enjoy aperitifs in the conservatory. It feels like home and you're even offered a second helping of the main course if you feel the urge. The cuisine fits the setting. It has few pretentions and perfects the tradition of Irish country food.

Jacobs on the Mall €€€ *30a South Mall, Cork, tel: (021) 425 1530, www.jacobsonthemall.com, open Mon–Sat 12.30–2.30pm, 6.30–10pm.* Local free-range and organic produce are used to create modern European dishes at this airy, contemporary restaurant in Cork City's financial district. There's also a piano bar.

Mary Ann's Bar and Restaurant €€ *Castletownshend, County Cork, tel: (028) 36146, www.westcorkweek.com/maryanns, open daily noon–2.30pm, 6–9pm; kitchen closed Mons Oct–Easter.* Seafood restaurant with cheaper menus served from the bar; the restaurant is set in a small, idyllic seaside village in West Cork. The bar dates back to 1846.

GALWAY

Ard Bia at Nimmo's €–€€ *Spanish Arch, Galway City, tel: (091) 561 114, café open Mon–Sat 9.30am–3.30pm, 6–10pm; restaurant Mon–Sat 6–10pm, Sun 10am–10pm, both closed Sun 5–6pm.* A stone warehouse building on Galway's quayside has a cheerful café with fresh organic food downstairs and a flamboyantly decorated restaurant upstairs serving more formal fare. Great food in a great atmosphere.

The Malt House €€ *Old Malt Arcade, 15 High Street, Galway City, tel: (091) 567 866, www.themalthouse.ie, open Mon–Sat noon–3pm, 5.30–10pm.* A quiet restaurant set in a charming old-world courtyard, but with cool and contemporary decor and a sophisticated menu of local seafood: try Galway Bay oysters with bacon and cabbage, or salmon in chilli broth.

McDonagh's Seafood House €–€€ *22 Quay Street, Galway City, tel: (091) 565 001, www.mcdonaghs.net, open Mon–Sat noon–11pm, Sun 5–11pm (fish and chips only).* Choose between freshly cooked traditional fish and chips or elaborately prepared local seafood, including lobster and scallops, at this long-established Galway institution.

Oyster Grill €€–€€€ *Hotel Meyrick, Eyre Square, Galway, tel: (091) 564 041, www.hotelmeyrick.ie, open for lunch 12.30–2.30pm and dinner 6.30–9.15pm.* Noted restaurant in centre of the city, serving first-class cuisine in uber cool surroundings.

KERRY

Chapter Forty €€€ *New Street, Killarney, tel: (064) 667 1833, www.chapter40.ie, open Mon–Sat 5–10pm.* Busy and stylish contemporary restaurant in town centre with award-winning chef. Locally sourced produce and a great buzz.

The Chart House €€ *The Mall, Dingle, tel: (066) 915 2255, www.charthousedingle.com, open Wed–Mon 6.30–10pm.* This informal, award-winning cottage restaurant has a warm welcome and high standard of cuisine highlighting freshly-landed fish and local artisan food.

Lime Tree Restaurant €€ *Shelbourne Street, Kenmare, tel: (064) 664 1225, www.limetreerestaurant.com, open daily 6.30–9.30pm.* Characterful premises in a converted schoolhouse host a serious restaurant serving mainstream and modern Irish cuisine. Wide-ranging menu and interesting wine list.

Park Hotel €€€ *Kenmare, tel: (064) 664 1200, www.parkkenmare. com, lounge menu served daily 11am–6pm, restaurant open daily 7–9pm.* One of Ireland's finest country house hotels, the Park's restaurant uses the finest local produce, prepared in classic French style, served in a relaxing dining area, with views over the lawns to the Caha Mountains.

LIMERICK AND SHANNON

Cullinan's Seafood Restaurant €€ *Doolin, County Clare, tel: (065) 707 4183, www.cullinansdoolin.com, open Easter–Oct Thur–Tue 6–9pm.* A simple, cottage restaurant attached to a small guest-house, Cullinan's serves fresh local produce, including Burren smoked salmon, Doolin crabmeat, Aran Island scallops, locally-raised lamb and beef, and Irish farmhouse cheeses.

Earl of Thomond Restaurant Dromoland Castle €€€ *New-market-on-Fergus, County Clare, tel: (061) 368 144, www.dromoland. ie, open daily 7–9.30pm, plus 12.30–1.30pm Sun.* The dining room in Dromoland Castle is spectacular, with superb, elaborate table settings and grand chandeliers overhead; excellent backdrop for the gourmet cuisine.

The Locke Bar and Bistro €–€€ *George's Quay, Limerick, tel: (061) 413 733, www.lockbar.com, open Mon–Sun 11am–12.30am.* Lively quayside gastropub with cheap and cheerful daily specials, an oyster bar and table service in the quieter upstairs restaurant.

The Mustard Seed at Echo Lodge €€€ *Newcastle West Road, Ballingarry, tel: (069) 68508, www.mustardseed.ie, open daily from 7pm.* Elegant four-course dining in a small Victorian country house hotel.

No. 1 Pery Square €€-€€€ *Pery Square, Limerick, tel: (061) 402 402, www.oneperysquare.com.* An imposing Georgian town house has been converted into a luxury hotel. Excellent bar food in gentleman's club-like surroundings, and more substantial fare in the first floor brasserie, Brasserie One.

WATERFORD

Cliff House Hotel €€€ *Ardmore, Co Waterford, tel: (024) 87800 www.thecliffhousehotel.com, Restaurant open Tue–Sat from 6pm, advance booking recommended.* Luxury boutique hotel with sensational cliff top setting and award-winning restaurant for serious foodies and lovers of high style.

O'Brien Chophouse €€, *Main Street, Lismore, Co Waterford, tel: (058) 53810, www.obrienchophouse.ie, open Weds–Sat 10.30am–9.30pm, Sun 11am–5pm.* Town centre pub converted into a cheerful restaurant, serving traditional Irish food, mainly organic and all sourced locally.

The Strand Inn €–€€ *Dunmore East, County Waterford, tel: (051) 383 174, www.dunmoreeast.com, open daily 6.30–10pm.* Situated beside a former smuggler's cove, this 300-year-old inn specialises in superb fresh seafood, seasonal produce and homemade desserts. There's also a lively pub with music.

The Tannery Restaurant €€€€ *10 Quay Street, Dungarvan, tel: (058) 45420, www.tannery.ie, open for dinner Tue–Fri 6–9.30pm, Sat 6.30–9.30pm, and lunch Fri 12.30–2.30pm and Sun 12.30–3pm.* One of the country's most stylish restaurants in a converted leather warehouse.

WEXFORD

Beaches at Kelly's Resort Hotel €€ *Rosslare, tel: (053) 32114, www.kellys.ie, open Sun–Fri 7.30–9pm, Sat 7–9pm.* Reservations are essential at this contemporary restaurant, as it's considered the place in which to be seen by the locals. The food is delicious, and the wine list is enticing.

Dunbrody Country House Hotel €€€ *Arthurstown, New Ross, tel: (051) 389600, www.dunbrodyhouse.com, open daily Mon–Sat 6.30–9.30pm, Sun 1.15–2.30pm.* A blend of classical Irish cooking and continental charm served in the Harvest Room, which overlooks an organic vegetable and fruit garden.

Marlfield House Hotel €€€ *Courtown Road, Gorey, tel: (053) 942 1124, www.marlfieldhouse.com, open daily, snack menu noon–5pm, dinner 7–9pm, Sun lunch noon–2pm.* The menu at this gorgeous and renowned country house is mainly classic French or Mediterranean with a twist. Fish, including wild salmon, Bannow Bay oysters and Wexford mussels, is a strong point. Fresh herbs, vegetables and fruit are picked from Marlfield's own gardens, which are popular with visitors. A delightful experience.

WICKLOW

The Hungry Monk €€ *Church Road, Greystones, tel: (01) 287 5759, www.thehungrymonk.ie, open Wed–Sat 6.30–11.30pm, Sun 5.30-11pm.* Intimate, candlelit restaurant in a seaside village, specialising in seafood in summer, wild game in winter. There's also a wine bar bistro here, open Mon–Sat 5–11pm and Sun 12.30–9pm.

Hunter's Hotel €€–€€€ *Newrath Bridge, Rathnew, tel: (0404) 40106, www.hunters.ie, open daily lunch 1–2.30pm, afternoon tea 4–5.30pm, dinner 7.30–9pm.* Hunter's Hotel is an historic 18th-century coaching inn with fine gardens. The food here is simple but impressive traditional Irish fare.

Kitty's of Arklow €€ *56 Main Street, Arklow, tel: (0402) 31669, open daily noon–5pm and 6–10pm.* This retro-style bar and restaurant stands in Arklow's town centre and is a local institution.

The Roundwood Inn €€ *Roundwood, tel: (01) 281 8107, open Fri–Sat 7.30–9pm, Sun 1–2pm.* Atmospheric old coaching inn serving local produce from lamb to venison. Good bar food, including goulash, Irish stew and smoked salmon.

NORTHERN IRELAND

Cayenne Restaurant ££ *7 Ascot House, Shaftesbury Square, Belfast BT2 7DB, tel: (028) 9033 1532, www.cayennerestaurant.co.uk, open lunch Tue–Fri noon–2.15pm, dinner Sun–Fri from 5pm and Sat from 6pm.* The reasonably priced fine food served at the Cayenne Restaurant has proved popular with Belfast's diners. There's a good wine list and a bar so stylish that you may forget you're waiting for a table.

Deane's Restaurant £££ *36–40 Howard Street, Belfast BT1 6PR, tel: (028) 9033 1134, www.michaeldeane.co.uk, open Mon–Sat noon–3pm and 6–10pm.* Deane's Restaurant offers one of the most memorable fine-dining experiences in Belfast in striking minimalist surroundings.

Madison's £–££ *59-63 Botanic Avenue, Belfast BT7 1JL, tel: (028) 9050 9800, www.madisonshotel.com.* The bistro menu (from 5pm) at this lively boutique hotel and bar features traditional Irish cuisine with a cosmopolitan twist.

Manor Park Restaurant ££ *2 College Hill, The Mall, Armagh, tel: (028) 3751 5353, www.manorparkrestaurant.co.uk, open Mon–Fri 10am–9.30pm, Sat 10am–5.30pm, Sun 10am–4pm.* French through and through (staff, menus, cuisine), albeit with a pride in local Irish ingredients, which are treated with care and cooked with skill by chef James Nelly.

The Percy French Pub and Bistro ££ *Hastings Slieve Donard Hotel, Downs Road, Newcastle, County Down BT33 0AH, tel: (028) 4372 1066, www.hastingshotels.com, open daily 10.30am–9.45pm.* A welcoming and popular venue, serving pub lunch and dinner fare. More formal meals in the Oak Room.

Portaferry Hotel ££ *The Strand, Portaferry, County Down BT22 1PE, tel: (028) 4272 8231, www.portaferryhotel.com, open daily 12.30–2.30pm, 5.30–6.30pm and 7–9pm.* The hotel is in a pleasant quayside spot and serves fresh seafood, including stuffed mussels, fried oysters and turbot. The pub serves good bar food.

A–Z TRAVEL TIPS

A Summary of Practical Information

A

ACCOMMODATION (See also Camping, Youth Hostels, and the selection of Recommended Hotels starting on page 134)

While exploring Ireland you can stay in different types of accommodation: a luxury hotel one night, a family-run guesthouse the next, or a farmhouse and thatched cottage. Efficient tourist offices will handle both spur-of-the-moment or long-range reservations for you in tourist board approved accommodatoin. Alternately, visit www.discoverireland.com for accommodation offers and good-value inclusive packages. Tariffs are government-controlled, and the maximum rate which proprietors may charge is displayed in all hotel rooms.

Hotel bills sometimes include a service charge, and you will find that VAT (value added tax) on the total cost of accommodation, meal and service is included in the rates.

Hotels and motels. These are graded by the tourist authorities into five-star ratings.

***** Most luxurious, highest standard of cuisine and services.

**** Extremely comfortable, with many amenities and fine dining.

*** Well-furnished, with private bath and many amenities.

** Well-kept, limited but good cuisine and service, most with private bath.

* Clean, comfortable, hot and cold running water, some ensuite.

The Irish Hotels Federation (www.irelandhotels.com) and the Northern Ireland Hotels Federation (www.nihf.co.uk) list associated hotels. B&B Ireland (www.bandbireland.com) is the major association of bed and breakfast providers. The Irish Self-Catering Federation (www.iscf.ie) and the Northern Ireland equivalant www.nischa.com) list registered providers, including thatched cottages.

AIRPORTS

International flights arrive at Dublin, Cork, Shannon, Knock and Belfast. Flights also operate from some UK airports to Kerry, Galway, Waterford, Donegal, City of Derry and Sligo.

Dublin Airport (DUB, tel: (01) 814 1111; www.dublinairport), 11km (7 miles) north of the Republic's capital, is the busiest. Coaches link the airport with Busaras, the city bus terminal, every 10–20 minutes. There is also a bus to Howth Junction railway station, provided by DART (Dublin Area Rapid Transit). This is the least expensive option. However you go, the trip takes between half an hour and an hour. Taxi time between the airport and central Dublin is also about half an hour.

Shannon Airport (SNN, tel: (61) 712 0000; www.snn.aero), one of the first Atlantic gateways, is situated about 24km (15 miles) to the west of Limerick.

Belfast International Airport (Aldergrove, BFS, tel: (028) 9448 4848; www.bial.co.uk) is 24km (15 miles) west of the city. A bus service to town operates every 30 minutes. **Belfast's George Best Airport** (BHD, tel: (028) 9093 9093; www.belfastcityairport.com) is handily situated near the city's old dockland area and mainly handles domestic and short-haul flights.

B

BICYCLE HIRE

See www.discoverireland.com/cycling for dealer contacts.

BUDGETING FOR YOUR TRIP

Average prices in euros with British pounds where applicable.

Accommodation: (based on bed and breakfast in a standard double room in low–high seasons) luxury hotel over €200 (£150)–midrange hotel €100–200 (£80–150); bed and breakfast €30–80 (£25–65).

Airport transfer: Dublin Airport to city centre by bus €6 (£4.50), by taxi €30 (£25) plus tip; Belfast International to city centre by bus £6, taxi £24; Belfast City Airport to city centre by bus £2.50, taxi £8.

Bicycle rental: about €75 (£60 per week, plus deposit).

Buses: local fares €4.30 (to the most distant suburb). An eight-day out of 15 Irish Rover ticket (bus only) covering both the Republic of Ireland and Northern Ireland is €190 (www.buseireann.ie), a five-day Tourist Rambler bus ticket for the greater Dublin area costs €22, three days is €13.50. Belfast Metro bus fares start from £1 for short journeys within the city up to £14 for a Smartlink Card giving you up to 10 journeys within the city and its outskirts.

Camping: around €9 (£7) per person per night for a tent pitch.

Entertainment: Cinema tickets cost around €9 (£7). Admission prices for nightclubs are €/£5–20 or more. Theatre tickets are €15–60 (£13–50).

Ferry: Galway–Aran Islands €25 roundtrip.

Meals and drinks: Expect to pay €25–65 (£20–54) per person for dinner with wine and coffee; up to €5.50 (£4.80) for a pint of Guinness, €5 (£4) for a pint of beer.

Museums, stately homes: €5–12 (£4.30–10).

Taxis: two-mile taxi journey in Dublin €10. You may find a supplement is payable for extra passengers, baggage, etc.

Tours: Dublin hop-on, hop-off bus tour €15. Bus tour around Ring of Kerry from Killarney €28. Belfast City Black Taxi Tour, £30 for up to two people (75 mins).

Trains: Dublin–Cork from €75 return.

C

CAMPING

Officially-approved campsites range from spartan to luxurious. Many a farmer will let campers stay on his property, but always ask first. At some campsites, and at rental agencies, touring caravans (trailers) can be rented. If pulling your own, note that the connections for Calor gas tanks are not suitable for the cylinders sold in Ireland. Lists of camping and caravanning parks and their facilities are available from tourist information offices or the Irish Caravan and Camping Council (www.camping-ireland.ie). Contact the Northern Ireland Tourist Board; tel: (028) 9023 1221; www.discover northernireland.com.

Horse-drawn caravans, most commonly found in west and south-west Ireland, can be rented by the week to sample the gypsy life. Book in advance through www.irishhorsedrawncaravans.com.

CAR HIRE (See also Driving in Ireland)

Car rental companies operate at airports and in towns. International firms usually have slightly higher rates than their local competitors. Some companies permit cars to be picked up in one place and returned elsewhere.

Most companies have a two-tiered tariff, raising prices by up to 20 percent for the summer season. In any season, cars may be rented on either a time-plus-mileage basis or with unlimited mileage, but if you're unsure whether you'll be chalking up enough travelling to justify the unlimited rate, the firm may agree to let you choose the more favourable tariff retroactively. Investigate before you travel.

A valid national licence, normally at least two years old, is required. Many firms permit 21-year-old drivers to rent cars, but the minimum age can be up to 25. The maximum age, depending on the company, ranges from 65 to 70. Credit cards are preferred.

Rentals begin at around €27 (£22) per day or €135 (£112) per week for a small car, including third party insurance, unlimited mileage and taxes. Add about €10 per day for collision damage waiver. Additional coverage can be arranged on the spot, and comprehensive coverage is recommended.

CLIMATE AND CLOTHING

The Gulf Stream is credited with keeping the Irish weather mild year-round, but the unexpected can happen with readings as cold as -19°C (-2°F) and as hot as 33°C (92°F) recorded over the past century. May is usually the sunniest month of the year, and December the dullest.

Temperatures do not vary much from north to south, but the weather in the west and southwest can be a good deal wetter than elsewhere because the winds come in direct from the sea. Pack some light protective clothing for the summer, and warmer items in the winter.

In the winter the Wicklow Mountains near Dublin, Donegal in the northwest and County Kerry in the southwest have heavy snowfalls, making the territory dangerous even for seasoned walkers and climbers. Wear warm, protective clothing, inform the hotel owners of your route and time of return and take some provisions with you. Average monthly temperatures in Dublin:

	J	F	M	A	M	J	J	A	S	O	N	D
°F	41	41	43	47	51	56	59	58	56	50	45	43
°C	5	5	6	8	11	13	15	14	13	10	7	6

CRIME (See also Emergencies and Police)

The Crime Prevention Office of the Garda Siochana (police) warns visitors to carry a minimum of cash and jewellery. Pickpockets do operate in shops and public places. Park in well-lit, busy areas.

D

DISABLED TRAVELLERS

A lot of progress has been made in recent years to provide more facilities for travellers with disabilities. Ramps have been provided, giving access to many community buildings, and much of the public transport system has been adapted. The more modern buses in Dublin have facilities for wheelchair users, and trains have level entry access.

DRIVING (See also Car Rental and Emergencies)

Drive on the left and give way to traffic from the right.

Taking your own car. Be sure to have the registration papers and insurance coverage. Virtually any valid driving licence from any country is recognised in Ireland. If yours doesn't include a photograph, keep your passport with you when driving.

Speed limits. Unless otherwise marked, the speed limit in the Irish Republic is 50km/h (30mph) in towns, 80km/h (50mph) on local roads, 100km/h (62mph) on national roads and dual carriageways and 120km/h (74mph) on motorways. In Northern Ireland: 30mph (50km/h) in towns, 60mph (86km/h) on local roads, and 70mph (44km/h) on national roads, dual carriageways and motorways.

Fuel. In some areas finding a petrol station open on a Sunday morning may be a problem, so it's best to top up on Saturday for weekend excursions. Petrol (gas) is sold by the litre.

Seat belts. Drivers and front-seat passengers must wear seat belts in the Republic and Northern Ireland; failure to use them may be punished by a fine. If a vehicle is built with rear seat belts, it is compulsory to use them.

Drinking and driving. Random breath tests are used in certain areas. Those who fail risk heavy fines or jail or both. This affects visitors as well as residents.

Road signs. The road direction signs in the Republic are mostly bilingual, in English and Gaelic. Road signs give distances in kilometres in the Republic and miles in Northern Ireland.

E

ELECTRICITY

The standard current everywhere is 220v, 50AC; hotels usually have special sockets for shavers, running at both 220 and 110v.

It is possible for certain appliances to need a converter, and also adapter plugs may be required to fit into Ireland's two types of wall outlets. These can be either three-pin flat or two-pin round.

EMBASSIES AND CONSULATES

Details of the principal embassies and consulates in **Dublin:**
Australia: Fitzwilton House, Wilton Terrace, Dublin 2; tel: (01) 664 5300; www.australianembassy.ie.

Canada: 7–8 Wilton Terrace, Dublin 2; tel: (01) 234 4000; www.canadaeuropa.gc.ca/ireland.

Great Britain: 29 Merrion Road, Dublin 4; tel: (01) 205 3700; www.britishembassyinireland.fco.gov.uk.

US: 42 Elgin Road, Dublin 4; tel: (01) 668 8777; http://dublin.usembassy.gov.

In Northern Ireland:

US: Danesfort House, 223 Stranmillis Road, Belfast BT9 5GR; tel: (028) 9038 6100; www.usembassy.org.uk/nireland.

EMERGENCIES (See also Embassies and Consulates and Health and Medical Care)

To contact the police, fire department, or an ambulance in the Republic or Northern Ireland, dial **999 or 112** and tell the emergency operator which service you need.

G

GAY AND LESBIAN TRAVELLERS

Nowadays the general attitude of younger people in Ireland tends to be tolerant towards gays and lesbians, but travellers may find there is a more conservative attitude in some of the more provincial or remote areas of the country.

Various organisations provide advisory services for gay people. They include the **Gay Switchboard** (www.gayswitchboard.ie), and the Dublin **Lesbian Line** (www.dublinlesbianline.ie).

GETTING THERE

From Great Britain
By Air

Visitors and tourists can fly in from airports across the UK to Dublin, Shannon, Cork, Kerry, Galway, Waterford, Donegal, Sligo and Knock in the Republic and to Belfast International, George Best (Belfast

City) and Derry airports in Northern Ireland. New routes are opening all the time, so do check with your airline.

Charter Flights and Package Tours. Some airlines offer fly-drive tours, or special fares including your flight and all the transport to and from your final destination in Ireland. Check with your airline.

Regional Flights. If your time in Ireland is short, you may consider domestic flights between regions. These are operated by Aer Arann, tel: (0870) 876 7676, www.aerarann.com; Aer Lingus, tel: (0871) 718 5000 (Ireland) or (0870) 876 5000 (UK), www.aerlingus.com; and Manx2, tel: (0871) 200 0400, www.manx2.com.

By Sea

Passenger and car ferries sail frequently from Britain to Ireland. There are services from: Holyhead to Dublin and Dún Laoghaire, Liverpool and Isle of Man to Dublin and Belfast, Fishguard and Pembroke to Rosslare, Cairnryan and Troon (Scotland) and Fleetwood (Lancashire) to Larne (near Belfast) and Stranraer to Belfast.

The main ferry operators include DFDS Seaways (www.dfdsseaways.com), Fastnet Line (www.fstnetline.com), Irish Ferries (www.irishferries.com), P&O Irish Sea (www.poirishsea.com), Stena Line (www.stenaline.co.uk) and Steam Packet Company (www.steampacket.com). Schedules and contact numbers are posted on the companies' websites.

From North America

By Air

Travellers from almost every major American city and several major Canadian cities can make connections to Dublin, Shannon, Belfast or Knock, either direct, or via New York, Chicago or Boston.

Charter Flights and Package Tours. Charter flights to Shannon, with connections to Dublin, feature even further air-fare reductions.

GUIDES AND TOURS

Guided tours are conducted at some major attractions as part of the admission fee, and a variety of excursions are led by guides, covering major monuments and beauty spots by bus. Tourist offices have schedules; the Dublin office at 88–95 Amiens Street, Dublin 1, tel: (01) 884 7700 has a list of qualified guides. See also www.discoverireland.com.

H

HEALTH AND MEDICAL CARE (See also Emergencies)

Residents of EU countries are covered by reciprocal health care in the Republic and in Northern Ireland, and visitors should be sure to bring their European Health Insurance Card (EHIC), which replaced the old E111 form. Other nationalities should have some form of medical insurance – most travel insurance policies provide adequate cover.

Hotels and pharmacies usually know which local doctors are available, but in an emergency dial **999 or 112** to find a doctor on call. The Dental Hospital, 20 Lincoln Place, Dublin 2, tel: (01) 612 7200, will treat emergency cases.

Pharmacies (chemists) operate during shopping hours. A few stay open until 10pm; in Belfast many are open on Sundays, while in the Republic only some are open for limited hours.

L

LANGUAGE

English is spoken everywhere in Ireland. In the Gaeltacht areas of the west and south, the principal language is Irish, though most people speak English too. Bilingualism is officially encouraged. For short language learning courses in the Gaeltacht, visit www.gaelsaoire.ie or tel: (1) 800 621 600 (Republic of Ireland) or 0800 783 5708 (UK). Here is a short Irish glossary to help you read the signs:

Irish/Gaelic	*English*
áth	ford of river
baile, bally	hamlet, group of houses, town

beann, ben	mountain peak
cairn	mound of stones atop a prehistoric tomb
carrick, carrig	rock
cather	fort
clachan, clochan	small group of dwellings; stepping stones across a river; beehive-shaped hut
corrach	marsh or low plain
derry, dare	oak tree or wood
donagh	church
drum, drom	ridge, hillock
dun, doon	fort
ennis, inch, innis(h)	island
kil, kill, cill	church; monk's cell
lough	lake, sea inlet
sceillig, skellig	crag, rock
sliabh, slieve	mountain
tulach, tully	hillock

Here are some handy phrases, with a rough guide to pronunciation:

Dia dhuit	hello	*diah guich*
slán	goodbye	*slawn*
oiche mhaith	good night	*e-ha wah*
go raibh maith agat	thank you	*goh rev moh a-gut*
le do thoil	please	*leh doh hol*
tá fáilte romhat	you're welcome	*taw faltcha rowet*
sláinte!	cheers!	*sloyn-tcha*
gam pardún	excuse me	*gum par-doon*
Cá bhuil an ...?	Where is the ...?	*koh will on*

M

MEDIA

Radio and Television. In the Republic, state-run Radio Telefís Éireann (RTE) is the largest broadcaster, though cable and digital television has expanded the choice and includes standard British stations. Most programmes are in English except for a few Irish or bilingual ones. RTE operates three radio stations mainly in English, TG4 in Irish, as well as Raidio na Gaeltachta with an all-Irish programme. In Northern Ireland, the BBC runs five radio stations and two TV stations alongside ITV and Channel Four.

Newspapers. Popular daily broadsheets are the *Irish Independent*, the *Irish Times* and the *Irish Examiner* and, in Northern Ireland, the *News Letter* and the *Belfast Telegraph*.

Entertainment news is covered in the *Evening Herald* of Dublin, the *Evening Echo* of Cork and the *Belfast Telegraph*. Sunday papers are also useful, and visitors will find a what's on section in the Friday edition of the *Irish Times*.

Irish editions of Britain's national daily and Sunday newspapers are sold almost everywhere in both countries on the morning of publication. Leading newsagents in the major towns also sell international newspapers and magazines.

MONEY

Currency. The unit of currency used in the Irish Republic is the euro (€); in Northern Ireland the British pound sterling (£) is used. Both are divided into 100 units. These units are called cents in the Republic, pence in the north. Euro banknotes are issued in €5, €10, €20, €50, €100 and also €500 denominations. Coins come in 1, 2, 5, 10, 20 and 50 cents and 1 and 2 euro.

Exchange facilities. All major banks and many building societies provide exchange facilities. Major post offices, including the GPO in Dublin, have a bureau de change. Some international travel agencies also change money and travellers' cheques. Be sure to take along your passport as proof of identity when cashing travellers' cheques (*see also page 126*).

The Suffolk Street Dublin Tourism Office and Ireland Southwest Tourism in Grand Parade, Cork, operate money exchange services.

Credit cards and travellers' cheques are widely accepted in Irish shops, hotels, restaurants and car-rental firms. Cash points at banks throughout the island offer cash advances on major cards.

○

OPENING HOURS

The opening hours of shops and offices can vary from season to season and according to where they are located.

Shops in the cities are normally open from 9am–6pm Mon to Sat and often on Sunday afternoons; country towns have one early closing day. Big shopping centres often stay open until 9pm on Thur and Fri. Smaller shops, particularly grocers and newsagents, often open on Sun and many stay open until 11pm.

Offices and businesses mostly operate from 9am–5.30pm Mon to Fri. Tourist information offices usually open from 9 or 10am–5pm with longer summer hours in the busiest places.

Banks. In general banks open 9.30am–4pm Mon to Fri in the Republic. Most towns stay open until 5pm on one day a week (Thur in Dublin). Northern Ireland banks keep similar hours, although outside Belfast, branches may close for lunch.

Pubs. In the Republic, the hours are generally 10.30am–11.30pm during the week, with an extra hour Thur–Sat. On Sun they can open at noon and stop serving at 11pm. In addition, there is half an hour drinking up time in the evenings all year round. In Northern Ireland, pubs are usually open Mon to Sat 11.30am–11pm, and on Sundays from 12.30–10pm, again with half an hour drinking up time. You may still find some pubs shut on a Sunday.

Museums and stately homes. Museums and stately homes follow no general rule except that visiting hours will often be curtailed in winter. There are no universal days when these institutions are closed, though Sun, Mon, or Tue are the most probable. To avoid disappointment always check first with the nearest tourist information office.

P

PHOTOGRAPHY

Be sure to ask permission before you take photos in museums and historic churches; sometimes flash is forbidden. Military bases (and installations of security forces in Northern Ireland) are off-limits to photographers.

POLICE (See also Emergencies)

The civic guard (police force) of the Irish Republic is the Garda Siochana, known as the Garda (pronounced 'gorda'). The Police Service of Northern Ireland performs similar duties in the North. In case of emergency, telephone 999 or 112, in both the Republic and Northern Ireland.

POST OFFICES

The Post operates all mail services offered in the Republic. Most mailboxes are pillar-shaped and painted green. Most post offices are open from 9am–5.30pm, but the main one – the historic General Post Office in O'Connell Street, Dublin – is open Mon–Sat 8am–8pm. Smaller post offices close from 1pm–2pm. Postcard shops and newsstands sometimes sell stamps too. In some areas a post office may be identified by a sign in Irish only – *Oifig an Phoist*.

In Northern Ireland the mailboxes are red. Note that Republic of Ireland stamps may not be used on mail posted in Northern Ireland and British stamps are invalid in the Republic.

PUBLIC HOLIDAYS

Banks and businesses are closed on public holidays, though some shops and restaurants may stay open. If a date falls on a Sunday, then the following Monday is taken in lieu.

In the Republic of Ireland and Northern Ireland:

1 January	*New Year's Day*
17 March	*St. Patrick's Day*

March/April (movable date)	*Good Friday/Easter Monday*
first Monday in May	*May Day*
25 December	*Christmas Day*
26 December	*Boxing Day*
In the Republic of Ireland only:	
first Monday in June	*June Bank Holiday*
first Monday in August	*August Bank Holiday*
last Monday in October	*October Bank Holiday*
In Northern Ireland only:	
last Monday in May	*Spring Bank Holiday*
12 July	*Orangemen's Day*
last Monday in August	*Summer Bank Holiday*

R

RELIGION

About 87 percent of the people in the Irish Republic are Catholic. Many but by no means all go to Sunday Mass, which can be heard in Dublin any time from 6am–9pm. Dublin's cathedrals are of the (Anglican) Church of Ireland, and schedules of the services at these and other Protestant churches can be found in hotels, and in Saturday papers. Dublin has Protestant, Greek Orthodox, Jewish and Islamic places of worship.

In Northern Ireland, Catholics make up just under half of the population, outnumbering the largest single Protestant group, the Presbyterians, as well as the Church of Ireland. The ecclesiastic capital of Ireland is Armagh, situated in the North with two cathedrals, one Catholic and the other Church of Ireland. Both are called St Patrick's.

T

TELEPHONES

Public telephones are found in post offices, hotels, stores and on the street. In the Republic sentry-box booths – cream with green trim –

and modern aluminium and glass booths are becoming increasingly hard to find as mobiles take over. They are marked in Gaelic, *Telefon*. In Northern Ireland, public telephones are found in metal and glass booths or yellow cubicles. They also generally accept coins and cards.

Most payphones in Ireland take pre-paid phone cards from local post offices and shops. Dial 10 for operator assistance.

Only mobiles with multi-band GSM will work in Ireland. It may be cheaper to buy a local SIM card and top up with prepaid calls. If you are coming from the UK your mobile should work in Northern Ireland. You will need international roaming in the Republic.

The international dialling code for the Republic of Ireland is 353, drop the initial zero of the local STD code or mobile number. Northern Ireland is 44 as it is part of the UK. The local code for Northern Ireland is 028, from the Republic you can dial 00 44 28 or simply dial 048 followed by the eight-digit number.

TIME ZONES

Ireland sets its clocks one hour ahead of GMT from mid-March to the end of October, but the rest of the year the clocks are set to GMT.

TIPPING

Some hotels and restaurants include a service charge, so tipping is unnecessary. If not, 10 percent of the bill in a restaurant and a couple of euros a day for cleaners is expected in both the Republic and Northern Ireland. Taxis are usually tipped by simply rounding up the fare.

TOILETS

Gender signs on doors in the Republic may be printed in Gaelic, not English. *Mná* is Gaelic for ladies; *fir* means gentlemen.

TOURIST INFORMATION OFFICES

Tourist information offices and Discover Ireland Centres all over Ireland provide full travel information and advice, booklets, maps and a comprehensive hotel reservation service (for a small charge). The offices are usually open from 9 or 10am–5 or 6pm, although many local ones operate only in the summer. For enquiries, contact:

Fáilte Ireland, 88 Amiens Street, Dublin 1, tel: (01) 884 7700, www.failteirealnd.ie, www.discoverireland.ie

Northern Ireland Tourist Board, St Anne's Court, 59 North Street, Belfast BT1 INB; tel: (028) 9023 1221; www.discovernorthern ireland.com. You may also address your enquiries to offices of the **British Tourist Authority** the world over, www.visitbritain.com.

TRANSPORT (See also Money)

Buses. The state-run Bus Éireann operates an extensive network of local, provincial and express bus routes in the Republic, including full cross-border services in conjunction with Northern Ireland's Ulsterbus Ltd. Services to tourist destinations increases in summer. Fares and schedule information can be downloaded from www.bus eireann.ie. Expressway buses provide a non-stop inter-city service, while Provincial vehicles make frequent stops in rural areas.

Dublin Bus (*Bus Atha Cliath*) runs services in the Dublin area. For information, tel: (01) 873 4222, www.dublinbus.ie. Dublin Area Rapid Transit (DART) provides a swift and frequent rail link through the city, from Howth in the north to Greystones in the south. For information on fares and schedules, see www.irishrail.ie/dart. The Luas tram system also provides light rail service to outlying suburbs, tel: 1800 300 604, www.luas.ie.

Bus Éireann sell Open Road passes allowing flexible cross-country travel for varying periods – eg three days out of six, right up to 15 days out of 30. There is also a Rover ticket, which allows up to 15 days of unlimited travel in the Republic, and includes the use of Ulsterbus in Northern Ireland. Or you can buy tickets for combined bus and rail travel: the Explorer pass, for example, is valid in the Republic only, while the Emerald Card can also be used in Northern Ireland.

Trains. Cross-country services to and from Dublin are both quick and comfortable. The main inter-city routes have air-conditioned, sound-proofed expresses. Super Standard (1st class) is only available on intercity Dublin-Cork trains. Irish Rail (*Iarnród Éireann*) operates trains in the Republic; tel: (1850) 366 222, www.irishrail.ie. In Northern Ireland, Translink operates Northern Ireland Railways, Enterprise (Belfast–Dublin train service), Ulsterbus (inter-urban), Metro bus (Belfast City) and Goldline (coach); tel: (028) 9066 6630; www. translink.co.uk. Train timetables are available at railway stations and tourist offices, and are also posted on the rail companies' websites.

Note: Dublin has two main-line railway stations (Heuston and Connolly), as well as a commuter-line station, so be sure to check in advance for the correct terminal.

Ireland is among the group of countries which are honouring the **Eurail Pass**, a flat-rate unlimited mileage ticket, valid for rail travel in Europe outside the UK and also the new Eurail Global Pass, which includes countries worldwide. Saver versions are available for those under 26.

Taxis. Most taxis park at designated stands waiting for clients. Many towns have radio-dispatched taxis or online booking, but these usually charge extra for the mileage to pick up the client. Fares can vary from town to town. Dublin and Cork have metered taxis while smaller towns have standard fares or charges by agreement.

Note that you should pay only the charge on the meter plus, if applicable, supplements for extra passengers, additional luggage, waiting time, and trips on public holidays or after midnight. An appropriate tip will be appreciated. Detailed receipts will be provided on request.

Boats and Ferries. With over 4,800km (3,000 miles) of coastline and 14,480km (9,000 miles) of rivers and streams, Ireland is a boater's paradise. You might rent a fishing boat to take advantage of the excellent fresh-water and sea fishing, or enjoy the country's scenic splendours in a rented cruiser (normally available with two to eight berths).

No boating permit is needed for travelling on the Shannon, and all companies offer a free piloting lesson. Points of departure include Carrick-on-Shannon, Athlone, Banagher and Killaloe.

The rugged islands off the coast of Ireland are rich in folklore, antiquities and eye-catching natural wonders (especially birdlife). Fáilte Ireland produces a free brochure, *Explore Islands of Ireland* listing numerous possibilities, including scheduled ferries. This information can also be found at www.discoverireland.ie. The Aran Islands are only a 20-km (30-mile) steamer ride from the Galway coast at Rossaveal, and crossings can also be made in May to September from Doolin in County Clare. Garinish Island, which is noted for its exuberant vegetation, is only 10 minutes away from Glengarriff (County Cork). Bad weather may interrupt ferry services. There are connections to the Aran Islands by air, as well; flights are around 10 minutes.

V

VISAS AND ENTRY REQUIREMENTS

Citizens of many countries do not require visas. EU citizens do not need a passport to enter Ireland, but most air and sea carriers require some form of photo identification, and some insist on a passport Non-UK nationals must have a valid passport or national ID card for stays of up to three months.

If you are coming from outside the euro zone, you must now fill in a Customs declaration form for cash sums of over €10,000 taken into or out of the Republic of Ireland.

If you are arriving in Ireland from another EU country, you can bring in the following items without paying further duties, as long as they are for personal use: 800 cigarettes, 200 cigars, 1kg of tobacco, 110 litres of beer, 90 litres of wine, 10 litres of spirits and 20 litres of fortified wine.

Residents of non-European countries can bring in 200 cigarettes or 50 cigars or 250g tobacco, plus 1 litre of spirits or 2 litres of fortified red wine, and 2 litres of wine plus 60ml perfume, 250ml eau de toilette and up to €175 worth of all other goods.

The customs restrictions between the Republic and Northern Ireland are normally limited to animals and agricultural products. There are no longer any border security checkpoints.

For more customs regulations information, visit www.revenue.ie.

WEBSITES

http://entertainment.ie Find out what's going on.
www.discovernorthernireland.com Northern Ireland Tourist Board.
www.heritageireland.ie Heritage of Ireland.
www.discoverireland.ie Irish Tourist Board.
www.goireland.com Reserve accommodation in hotels, B&Bs and hostels.

YOUTH HOSTELS

The Irish Youth Hostels Association runs 27 hostels in the Republic of Ireland. Membership cards are required, and these are issued by national youth hostel associations overseas. An official handbook is available from the **An Óige (HO),** 61 Mountjoy Street, Dublin 7; tel: (01) 830 4555; www.anoige.ie. **Independent Hostels of Ireland**, (tel: (74) 973 0130 for a brochure or see www.independent hostelsireland.com) is an association of hostel owners with no membership or age requirements and no curfew. There are some 67 hostels throughout Ireland.

There are six youth hostels in Northern Ireland. Ask for details from **Hostelling International Northern Ireland**, 22–32 Donegall Road, Belfast BT12 5JN; tel: (028) 9032 4733; www.hini.org.uk.

Recommended Hotels

A wide variety of accommodation can be found in Northern Ireland and the Republic. Bed and breakfast can cost as little as €24 (£20) per person per night. For €60 (£50) a night, hotels can be luxurious. Those registered with Tourism Ireland have guaranteed standards. Self-catering accommodation is widespread, though you will have to book well in advance during the peak summer months. The international star system awards top hotels 5 stars, and 1 star to modest hotels. Guesthouses get 1 to 4 stars. Local tourist information offices have details of offers in their area. Hotel prices are subject to 9 percent VAT in the Republic; 17.5 percent in Northern Ireland.

Price categories below are for a standard double room in high season (some include breakfast – check when you book). Please bear in mind that prices can be much cheaper and deals are often available:

€€€ over €200   £££ over £150
€€ €100–200   ££ £80–150
€ under €100   £ under £80

DUBLIN

Aberdeen Lodge €€ *55 Park Avenue, tel: (01) 283 8155, www. halpinsprivatehotels.com.* A large Victorian house in the elegant embassy quarter with quiet, spacious bedrooms beautifully furnished. A five-minute bus or DART ride to the city centre.

Bewley's Hotel Ballsbridge € *Merrion Road, tel: (01) 668 1111, www.bewleyshotels.com.* An excellent value hotel next to the RDS Arena with over 300 rooms at a flat rate, and a lively lounge bar. Ample car parking onsite, and a five-minute bus or DART ride to the city.

Blooms Hotel €–€€ *6 Anglesea Street, Dublin 2, tel: (01) 671 5622, www.blooms.ie.* Located in the Temple Bar area, and like most hotels here, there's a stylish restaurant, bar and basement nightclub to keep you entertained most of the night.

Buswells Hotel €€ *23–27 Molesworth Street, Dublin 2, tel: (01) 614 6500, www.buswells.ie.* Centrally located just opposite the National Museums complex, Buswells is set in a former Georgian townhouse and a favourite haunt of Dublin politicians. Most come just for the restaurant and bar.

Central Hotel €–€€ *1–5 Exchequer Street, Dublin 2, tel: (01) 679 7302, www.centralhotel.ie.* Around for over 100 years and housed in a rambling, refurbished Victorian building with a location as central as its name. The first floor Library Bar attracts literary types.

Clarence Hotel €€€ *6–8 Wellington Quay, Dublin 2, tel: (01) 407 0800, www.theclarence.ie.* Once upon a time this was simply a happy home for clergy up from the country on business. Now it's owned by U2 members and its Octagon bar is one of the most popular meeting places in Dublin. The hotel itself is decked out with Irish craftsmanship that's contemporary yet reminiscent of that country's past.

Conrad Dublin €€€ *Earlsfort Terrace, Dublin 2, tel: 602 8900, www.conraddublin.com.* Situated just off St Stephen's Green, the Conrad is the first stop for travelling royalty, though the service seems to roll out the red carpet for all guests. It's most popular for business people but the pub attracts Dubliners.

Dublin International Youth Hostel € *61 Mountjoy Street, Dublin 7, tel: 830 1766, www.anoige.ie.* Budget-priced accommodation in a converted convent.

The Morrison, €€€ *Lower Ormond Quay, Dublin 1, tel:887 2400, www.morrisonhotelie.* City-centre quayside hotel that vies with the Clarence (see above) for title of most media-hip hotel in town. Contemporary design and good location.

O'Callaghan Davenport Hotel €–€€€ *Merrion Square, Dublin 2, tel: (01) 607 3500, www.ocallaghanhotels.com.* An elegant lemon-coloured building dating from the 1860s and set amidst the attractions of Merrion Square.

The Shelbourne €€€ *27 St Stephen's Green, Dublin 2, tel: (01) 663 4500, www.theshelbourne.ie.* Once home to the Irish Constitution (it was written here), it is now home to Dublin's more distinguished visitors. You couldn't ask for more than a room overlooking St Stephen's Green, but the popularity of the Horseshoe Bar with Dublin's glitterati will give you even more to look at.

Staunton's on the Green €€ *83 St Stephen's Green South, Dublin 2, tel: (01) 478 2300, www.stauntonsonthegreen.ie.* Exclusive Georgian guesthouse overlooking the green with spacious rooms and delightful period decor.

The Westbury €€€ *Grafton Street, Dublin 2, tel: (01) 679 1122, www.doylecollection.com.* A luxury city centre hotel that knows best how to cater to business visitors, though with this location, leisure guests will never need walk far to the city's attractions.

Wynn's Hotel €€ *35–39 Lower Abbey Street, Dublin 1, tel: (01) 874 5131, www.wynnshotel.ie.* This city-centre hotel is just around the corner from the Abbey Theatre.

MEATH

The Millhouse €€€ *Slane, County Meath, tel: (041) 982 0723, www.themillhouse.ie.* Romantic Georgian manor with sumptuous four posters, log fires and the beautiful River Boyne as a backdrop.

CORK

Ambassador Hotel €€ *Military Hill, St Luke's, Cork, tel: (021) 453 9000, www.ambassadorhotelcork.ie.* An imposing Victorian building converted into a stylish, hill-top hotel, with great views of the city and harbour. Both bar and restaurant have a lively local trade.

Ballymaloe House €€€ *Shangarry, Midleton, tel: (021)465 2531, www.ballymaloe.ie.* One of Ireland's leading country-house hotels, Ballymaloe is a stylishly decorated Georgian house surrounded by the family farm. Renowned for its restaurant, which pioneered the imaginative use of fresh local produce. Children welcome.

Blue Haven Hotel €€ *3 Pearse Street, Kinsale, tel: (021) 477 2209, www.bluehavenkinsale.com.* The hotel's individually-styled rooms are well planned but compact, with the type of space you'd expect in a city-centre hotel. There is a fine bar and coffee shop to retire to, and the location couldn't be better.

Seaview House Hotel €€ *Ballylickey, Bantry Bay, tel: (027) 50073, www. seaviewhousehotel.com*. Set in extensive grounds on the shores of Bantry Bay, this Victorian manor house is now a comfortable, family-run, country-house hotel, with an excellent restaurant. A good base for touring the southwest.

GALWAY

The G Hotel €€€ *Wellpark, Galway, tel: (091) 865200, www.theg hotel.ie*. Milliner Phillip Treacey has designed a hotel that, like his hats, is quirky, extravagant and luxurious. Kick back in the cool restaurant and bar or chill out in the soothing spa.

Hotel Meyrick €€–€€€ *Eyre Square, Galway, tel: (091) 564041, www. hotelmeyrick.ie*. Historic 19th-century railway hotel located in the heart of the city. There's no lack of old Irish charm here but a swish new makeover means it draws a trendy crowd these days. The Oyster Bar has a wide selection of drinks and an impressive cocktail list.

KERRY

Greenmount House €€ *Upper John Street, Dingle, tel: (066) 915 1414, www.greenmounthouse.ie*. Only a short walk from the busy town centre, this quiet 14-room guesthouse has a great view of the sunset over Dingle. Rooms are spacious and contemporary and the breakfast is renowned.

Lake Hotel €–€€ *Muckross Road, Killarney, tel: (064) 31035, www. lakehotelkillarney.com*. The grounds of this large, rambling, country hotel run right down to the lakeshore and adjoin Killarney National Park, putting you right in the middle of the Killarney experience. There's an outdoor hot tub on the lakeshore, which is part of a fitness centre.

Parknasilla Resort €€€ *Sneem, Ring of Kerry, tel: (064) 667 5600, www.parknsillahotel.ie*. Set in a sheltered inlet with sub-tropical vegetation with a mountain backdrop, this is the ultimate getaway. Excellent pool and spa, old-fashioned lounge and bar, and self-catering options for families.

Sheen Falls Lodge €€€ *Kenmare, tel: (064) 41600, www.sheenfalls lodge.ie.* A 120-hectare (300-acre) estate and waterside setting comes along with a room in this lodge. The lounge bar welcomes you in with a roaring fire and gives you a view of the spilling waterfall outside. Spacious rooms offer views of the river or Kenmare Bay. There is also an equestrian centre, library and nature walk through the woodland.

KILKENNY

Club House Hotel €€ *Patrick Street, Kilkenny, tel: (056) 772 1994, www.clubhousehotel.com.* Historic 18th-century hotel; mementoes include a set of witty 19th-century political cartoons.

Hotel Kilkenny €€–€€€ *College Road, Kilkenny, tel: (056) 776 2000, www.griffingroup.ie.* Newly refurbished hotel just outside the city with bedrooms, including some family rooms, in a light, contemporary design.

LIMERICK AND SHANNON

Carlton Castletroy Park Hotel €€–€€€ *Dublin Road, Limerick, tel: (061) 335566, www.castletroy-park.ie.* One of Limerick's most sought after hotels for conference facilities, but still capable of rolling out a proper welcome to leisure guests. Enjoy some relaxation at the Aqua and Fitness club or pamper yourself at the Blue Door Salon.

Dromoland Castle €€€ *Newmarket-on-Fergus, County Clare, tel: (061) 368144, www.dromoland.ie.* This luxury estate can trace its heritage back to Gaelic royalty via the O'Briens, once barons of Inchiquin, who were direct descendants of Brian Boru. Despite all this history, the hotel is welcoming, relaxing and mystical – especially the grounds of the castle which include a lake and delightful parklands.

Fitzgerald's Woodlands House Hotel €–€€ *Knockanes, Adare, County Limerick, tel: (061) 605100, www.woodlandshotel.ie.* A lively,

modern hotel just outside the village, this is a good base for touring the Shannon region. There's a new leisure centre and spa, and a
choice of two popular restaurants.

Gregan's Caslte €€€ *Ballyvaughan, County Clare, tel: (065) 707
7005 www.gregans.ie.* One of Ireland's leading country house hotels
in extensive gardens with breathtaking views over Galway Bay. An-
tique furniture and contemporary art and an outstanding restaurant
– but only one TV in the house.

Sleepzone € *The Burren, Doolin Road, Lisdoonvarna, County Clare,
tel: (091) 566 999, www.sleepzone.ie.* This comfortable good value
hostel opened in March 2007 in a former hotel in the lively village
of Lisdoonvana.

MAYO

Ashford Castle €€€ *Cong, County Mayo, tel: (094) 954 6003, www.
ashford.ie.* The last word in luxury accommodation, this former 19th-
century mansion of the Guinness family is arguably Ireland's grand-
est castle hotel, with parts dating back to the early 13th century. The
best rooms are at the top of the castle and offer views of Lough Corrib, the River Cong and the surrounding parkland.

Boffin Lodge € *The Quay, Westport, tel: (098) 26092, www.boffinlodge.
com.* Small and stylish traditional-style guesthouse in a tranquil location near Westport's quays, half a mile from the town centre. There
are four-poster beds and steam rooms available. Close to a good
choice of pubs and restaurants.

Quiet Man Hostel € *Abbey Street, Cong, County Mayo, tel: (094) 954
6846, www.quietman-cong.com.* The hostel, aka Michaeleen's Manor,
offers budget accommodation located close to pubs, shops, the river
and Cong Abbey.

WATERFORD

Granville Hotel €€ *Meagher Quay, Waterford, tel: (051) 305555,
www.granville-hotel.ie.* Situated along Waterford's quayside and with

as many historical connections as rooms, it's very popular with business travellers but makes a great base for exploring the town.

Rice Guest House €–€€ *35 Barrack Street, Waterford, tel: (051) 371606, www.riceguesthouse.com.* Family-run guesthouse, a two-minute walk from the city centre, with a restaurant, bar and entertainment five nights a week.

Richmond House €€ *Cappoquin, County Waterford, tel: (058) 54278, www.richmondhouse.net.* Beautiful country house with spacious rooms and period furnishings set in scenic grounds. Excellent restaurant serving Irish and French cuisine.

Waterford Castle €€€ *The Island, Ballinakill, Waterford, tel: (051) 878203, www.waterfordcastle.com.* Historic castle situated on its own private island on the River Suir, surrounded by woodlands and an 18-hole championship golf course. 19 bright and airy bedrooms with stunning views of the estate.

WEXFORD

Ferrycarrig Hotel €€€ *Wexford, tel: (053) 912 0999, www.ferrycarrig hotel.ie.* Each of the large, stylish rooms has a splendid view of the River Slaney estuary. Excellent riverside restaurant, bar, spa and leisure activities. Outside Wexford town and convenient for the Irish National Heritage Park.

Kelly's Resort Hotel and Spa €€€ *Rosslare, County Wexford, tel: (053) 913 2114, www.kellys.ie.* Located on sandy Rosslare beach, this is one of Ireland's great family-run hotels, with an excellent restaurant and spa.

NORTHWEST

Green Gate € *Ardvalley, Adara, County Donegal, tel: (074) 954 1546, www.thegreengate.eu.* This traditional cottage was bought by the proprietor as a writer's retreat. He's now made it a home away from home for himself and all those lucky enough to spend this night atop a hill on the edge of the Atlantic.